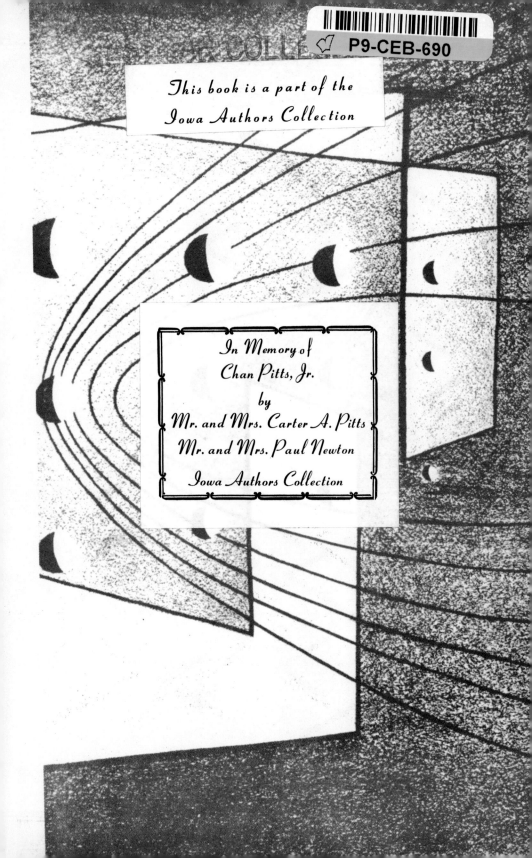

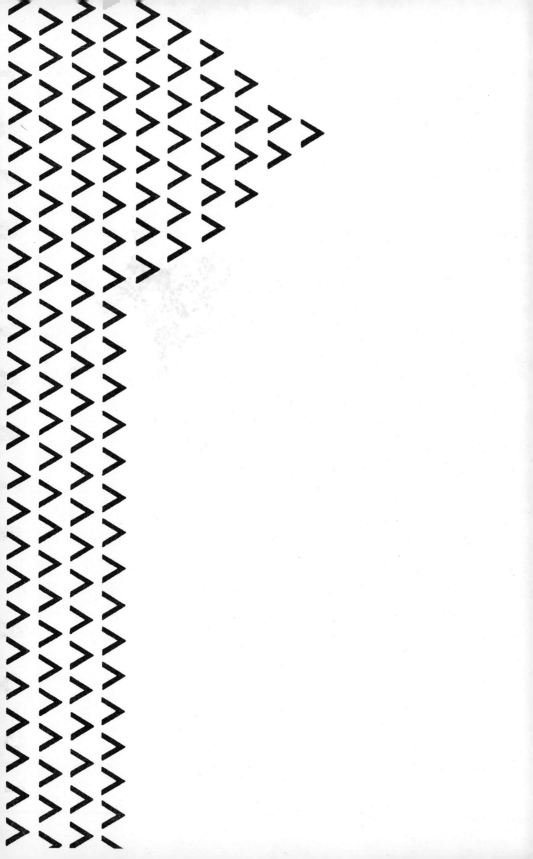

A

Merle Armitage

Book

Igor
Strav

Edited by

Essay Index Reprint Series

WORKS OF ART BY:

Pablo Picasso • Russell Cowles

Edward John Stevens Jr. • Paul Klee

Cady Wells • Marc Chagall

Carlus Dyer • Antonio Frasconi

P. G. Napolitano • J. E. Blanche

Arnold Newman • Fred Plaut

Edward Weston • John Vachon

insky

EDWIN CORLE

BOOKS FOR LIBRARIES PRESS

FREEPORT, NEW YORK

Copyright 1949 by Merle Armitage

Reprinted 1969 by arrangement

Articles and Essays by:

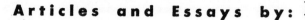

BORIS DE SCHLOEZER

ERIK SATIE

EUGENE GOOSSENS

JEAN COCTEAU

HENRY BOYS

AARON COPLAND

ARTHUR BERGER

NICOLAS NABOKOFF

MERLE ARMITAGE

EDWIN CORLE

ROBERT CRAFT

SIR OSBERT SITWELL

SAMUEL DUSHKIN

CECIL SMITH

LAWRENCE MORTON

DAVID HALL

STANDARD BOOK NUMBER:

8369-1120-2

LIBRARY OF CONGRESS CATALOG CARD NUMBER:

77-84295

PRINTED IN THE UNITED STATES OF AMERICA

C O N T E N T S

Contents

Block Print By Antonio Frasconi

1

E D W I N   C O R L E

1949   **Editor to Reader**

The first book ever printed in English on the music of Igor Stravinsky was a symposium of eleven commentaries collected by Merle Armitage and published in New York in 1936. During the thirteen years that have passed a great deal more has become known about the music of Stravinsky, and a great deal more of it exists now than was available for critical commentary in 1936.

This book contains five of the critiques from the 1936 volume, as it seemed to Mr. Armitage and to me that these five approaches were consistently sound, albeit technically different, and that what the authors had to say should not be allowed to disappear into the limbo of the out-of-print. These five pieces are by Eugene Goossens, Jean Cocteau, Erik Satie, Henry Boys, and Boris de Schloezer. The article by de Schloezer is a translation by Ezra Pound.

This present volume contains fifteen critiques ranging from the casual through the technical to the intimate and the personal. All facets of Stravinsky and his art are analyzed and commented upon from some points of view that may be emotional, to others that are purely scholarly. The reader will be enlightened and perhaps amused at the diversities presented by fifteen candid and honest points of view.

Everyone has some definite approach, and, as I said in a previous comment on the 1936 volume, it is extremely interesting to see why the work of a complex artist like Stravinsky can be called in different essays, at once "a mystical attitude" and "dynamic realism" — and the reader will find other provocative anomalies. They are not, however, the ambiguities of muddiness and uncertainty, but rather the essentially variegated conclusions inevitable in analyzing the complex career of this genius.

The reader will complete this book his own critic of Stravinsky, and his criticism will be the eclectic result of the reactions of fifteen critical minds. In its very liberality of point of view lies one of the book's claims to distinction.

Another interesting attempt by Mr. Armitage has been the inclusion in both the 1936 and the present volume of reproductions of the works of modern painters — Pablo Picasso, Cady Wells, Carlus Dyer, Paul Klee and others. These are in no sense interpretive, but their originality and freedom serve to show parallel directions in another art form that may assist in explanation of Stravinsky to those music lovers he confounds.

Also there are a number of striking portraits of Stravinsky by Russell Cowles, Marc Chagall, P. G. Napolitano and Pablo Picasso in which vitality, clarity, and precision, are realized to a degree comparable to Stravinsky's own art.

As a unit this latest book on the work of a man posterity may call the world's greatest composer is comprehensive but not definitive. All of the authors appreciate the genius, but the full values come through the varieties of approach. This is not a book to settle a discussion about Stravinsky; it is a book to begin one.

2

J E A N   C O C T E A U

1922   Critics and the Comic Spirit

From the sea-side, where I have come for a rest, Igor Stravinsky's last adventure presents itself with a simplicity and relief which makes it easily comprehensible at once.

The critics and the Parisian public, having grown accustomed to L'OISEAU DE FEU, received PETRUCHKA very badly when it first appeared; then, when they had got accustomed to PETRUCHKA, they hissed LE SACRE DU PRINTEMPS. Today, accustomed to LE SACRE, they are sulky about MAVRA.

Stravinsky has indeed, a well-planted mind. I mean by that, well-planted as well-brushed hair is well-planted — with just the right amount of hair on each side of the part. There is no disorder in this Slavic genius. He sounds his organs, takes care of his muscles and never loses his head. He knows that an artist who spends his whole life in the same costume ceases to interest us. Consequently, he transforms himself, changes his skin and emerges new in the sun, unrecognizable by those who judge a work of art by its outside.

After L'OISEAU DE FEU, in which one felt the influences of Rimsky and Wagner, came the mysterious, picturesque, highly coloured, profoundly disturbing PETRUCHKA. After PETRUCHKA came LE SACRE DU PRINTEMPS, which shot up in the orchestra before our very eyes like a tree in one of those moving picture films that shows plants growing at such a terrific rate. LE SACRE is harsh, sad, stark, stubborn, like the beginning of the ages. But just as Bayreuth established a sort of extra-musical religious atmosphere, which brought to earth the reign of the paste-board sublime, just so does LE SACRE by its grandeur and its power bring a sort of simplicity among the initiated — quite different from the other, to be sure, but also dangerous for young musicians. However, a work like LE SACRE, a really monster work, is always dangerous. Dangerous for others and dangerous for the author. A disorderly genius, with a badly planted intelligence, happening to give birth to such a work, would be likely

22

to stop there, to make capital of it his whole life, as if it were a gold mine.

See how Stravinsky escapes from this situation. I have not heard MAVRA but I get a very good idea of it from reading the unfavorable criticisms. A composition by Stravinsky never gives the critics what they expect of it. What do they expect? A work which resembles the one before it or perhaps something so vague, so mediocre, that a great man would never be able to produce it. On this occasion, the NOCES would perhaps have cajoled them, for the NOCES, which precedes MAVRA and RENARD (another misunderstood and perfect work) is descended in a straight line from PETRUCHKA and LE SACRE. But choral difficulties have transposed the chronological order of productions, and we shall hear the NOCES later.

Our brave post-impressionists, who have already been disturbed by LE SACRE in the midst of their sonorous little musicale, on this occasion virtuously refused to allow themselves to be led into a resort of ill-fame, that is to say, into our camp. Think of it! Stravinsky bringing the homage of his supreme contribution to the endeavors of Satie and our young musicians. Stravinsky the traitor. Stravinsky the deserter. It would never occur to any of them to think: Stravinsky the Fountain of Youth. For, no one ever gives the masters credit. It would be simple to say to one's self, "He is stronger than I. His instinct is surer. He must be right. It would be wise to

follow him!" No. Everybody thinks, "He is mistaken and I —
clever fellow — am the only person who knows it." This down-
pour of drivel, of lava and ashes, is, however, a good thing for
a work. Thus, the critics think to destroy it, but they only cover
it up, they protect it and preserve it, and a long time afterwards
an excavation brings the marble to light, intact.

ERIK   SATIE

1923   A Composer's Conviction

I have always said — and shall continue to repeat long after
my demise — that there is no such thing as truth in art (that
is, no single or absolute truth).

The truth of Chopin, that prodigious creator, is not the
truth of Mozart, that luxurious musician, whose writing is
imperishable scintillation; neither is Gluck's truth that of Pergolesi; nor is the truth of Liszt that of Haydn, which when all
is said, is very lucky.

If there be such a thing as one artistic truth, where does it
begin? Who is the master who possesses it in its entirety? Is
it Palestrina? Is it Bach? Is it Wagner?

25

When I hear it said that there is one truth in art this statement seems as astounding to me as a proclamation that such things exist as a locomotive-truth, a house-truth, an aviator-truth, an emperor-truth, a beggar-truth, etc.; and no one dreams of formulating, at least publicly, such a principle (out of modesty, perhaps, or possibly out of common sense); for it is very important not to confound a "type" even a very real one, with the truth.

However, the critics who specialize in the different arts, are inclined to present the public with idea-truths, which they defend with all the weight of their sumptuous knowledge and their authorized competence.

They do it without *parti pris,* of that I am convinced, but still they go on doing it, and have for centuries, the good souls (relieving each other, of course); it has now, doubtless become a habit.

Let these gentlemen allow me to disagree with them in as friendly a way as possible; I hope they will permit me the right of not sharing their conviction on this subject.

I shall not cease to repeat, night and day: "There is no truth in art."

My illustrious friend Igor Stravinsky, of whom I am going to speak, is the living proof of this; he is also its most precise, real and appropriate example.

Igor Stravinsky was born in Oranienbaum near Petrograd, the fifth (eighteenth O. S.) of June, 1882. His father, an opera

FEU D'ARTIFICE, pour orchestre (1908); CHANT FUNEBRE SUR LA MORT DE RIMSKY-KORSAKOV (1908); QUATRE ETUDES pour piano (1908); DEUX MELODIES (Gorodetzky-1908); L'OISEAU DE FEU, Conte danse (1909-10); SUITE DE L'OISEAU DE FEU pour orchestre; BERCEUSE DE L'OISEAU DE FEU, pour petit orchestre; BERCEUSE ET FINAL DE L'OISEAU DE FEU, pour petit orchestre; DEUX MELODIES (Verlaine-1910); PETROUSCHKA, Scenes burlesques en 4 tableaux (1910-21); SUITE DE PETROUSCHKA, pour ochestre; DEUX MELODIES (Balmont — choeur d'hommes avec orchestre-1911); LE SACRE DU PRINTEMPS, tableau de la Russie Paienne (1911-13); TROIS MELODIES DE LA LYRIQUE JAPONAISE, pour une voix de femme et neuf instruments (bois, piano et cordes-1912); SOUVENIR DE MA JEUNESSE, trois melodies enfantiles pour chant et piano (1913); LE ROSSIGNOL, opera en 3 actes (1909-14); LE CHANT DU ROSSIGNOL, poeme symphonique d'apres les deuxieme et troisieme actes de l'Opera Le Rossignol (1917); TROIS PIECES FACILES, pour piano a 4 mains (Main Gauche Facile-1915); CINQ PIECES FACILES, pour piano a 4 mains (Main Droite Facile-1917); BERCEUSES DU CHAT, suite de chants pour une voix de femme et 3 clarinettes (Mises en Francais par C. F. Ramuz — 1915-16); PRIBAOUTKI, chansons plaisantes pour une voix & huit instruments (Mises en Francais par C. F. Ramuz-1914); RENARD, histoire burlesque en un acte, pour 4 voix d'hommes et orchestre (Mises en Francais par C. F. Ramuz — 1916-17); LES NOCES VILLAGEOISES, scenes russes en 2 parties avec chant et musique (Mises en Francais par C. F. Ramuz-1917); MAVRA, ouvrage lyrique (which the Russian Ballet has just presented at the Paris Opera).

28

I now want to try to reveal to you the spirit of this work, the extent of which you have just seen. But I must hasten to announce that I do not intend to write a criticism of it; I shall content myself by giving a description of Stravinsky's splendid and fairy-like talent.

One of the characteristics of Stravinsky's music is the "transparency" of his sound. This is a quality that one always finds in the purists, who never leave any "residuum" in their sonority, that residuum which you will ever encounter in the musical fabric of impressionistic composers and also, alas! even in that of the Romantics.

Palestrina makes us "hear" this sonorous "transparency"; he was an expert manipulator of it and seems to have been the first to import this phenomenon into music.

The exquisite Mozart used it in a way that defies analysis. One stands confounded before such mastery, such a subtle "clairvoyance" of sound, a phonic lucidity so calm and so perfect.

Any one of Igor Stravinsky's works will cause you to perceive with extraordinary clearness this vibratory "transparency" of which I speak. LE SACRE DU PRINTEMPS is full of it; and it is perhaps in this work that it will appear to you with the most persuasiveness; you will be prodigiously bathed in it, deeply saturated.

Although Stravinsky knows that perfection is not of this world, he seeks continually to capture it, to subject it. If he is meticulous and exacting in his demands on the interpreters of his compositions, he gives them the example of his own careful conscientiousness. To see him at a rehearsal is an excellent lesson, for he knows what he wants and is keenly alive to what means of expression are at his disposal.

The master of an amazing dynamism, he shakes the masses, waking them from their apathy. To his play with "dynamism" he brings balance and precision; above all, no pedantry. And what color in his voluntary chaos! Stravinsky shows us the whole richness of his musical power in his use of dissonance. There he finally reveals himself and intellectually inebriates us. What a marvelous magician!

For him dissonance is emphasis and it is through it that he impresses the sensibility of a trained hearer. His dissonance is in no way hard; it manifests itself like a stream, always undulating, always adapting itself to and furthering the main current of his content.

Stravinsky's method of orchestration is novel and bold. He never orchestrates mushily; carefully skirting "holes" in composition and that "fog" which wrecks as many musicians as it does mariners. He always heads directly where he intends to go.

It should be noted that Stravinsky's orchestration is the result of a profound and exact instrumentation. His whole "orchestra" is built on the instrumental "timbre." Nothing is left to chance. Whence has he drawn his own sumptuous "truth"?

See in him a remarkable logician, sure and energetic; no one has ever written with more magnificent power, with a firmer assurance, with a more constant will.

I should reproach myself if I did not quote the following passage from an article by M. Ernest Ansermet:

"Stravinsky has told no one of the sacrifices which his musical evolution has demanded of him; he has had to let all sorts of musical habits go by the board, to discard all sorts of loyalties to beloved forms, all sorts of easy roads which he might have taken. His evolution is not the result of a deliberate plan; rather has it been imposed upon him by the pitiless logic of his creative genius. The end of this evolution is a graft on the savage, but, from whatever point we view it, is not this grafting justified?"

I love and admire Stravinsky because I perceive also that he is a liberator. More than anyone else he has freed the musical thought of today, which was sadly in need of development.

I am glad to have to recognize this, I who have suffered so much from the Wagnerian oppression, or rather that of the Wagnerians. For, a few years ago, the genius of Wagner was miserably adored by the combined Mediocrity and Ignorance of the crowd.

You can imagine how difficult it was to be a Wagnerian, even for a joke; it was only necessary to say in a loud voice: "Ah, how beautiful!" and one was immediately taken for a savant or an imbecile.

Every day I saw Cesar Franck ridiculed; at that time he was considered nonexistent. Chabrier was misunderstood and dubbed an amateur. Wagner's dictatorship was the sole power and odiously dominated the general taste. An era of desolation, during which the great classics themselves seemed blasted.

For many long years we have endured the sort of persecution which was brought in the old days against what was then called "decadent" poetry, that persecution organized by the literary partisans of the lesser Romanticism, who used the name of Victor Hugo as their battle cry; we musicians have endured, in our later turn, the same bitternesses, vexations and discouragements which were the lot of Baudelaire, Verlaine, Mallarme and the other poets.

But, today things have changed: — a happy sunlight illumines the recesses of our souls.

I do not know what I am myself, but, what I do know is that the man I have been telling you about is one of the greatest musicians who ever lived.

4

B O R I S   D E   S C H L O E Z E R

1928   An Abridged Analysis

(Translated by Ezra Pound)

. . . Interviewed by a Russian journalist, Stravinsky once condemned Scriabine as "a being devoid of all national character. He hasn't a passport. One must have a passport." . . .

It is now ten years since the composer abandoned the so vast domain of Russian popular song, from which he had for so long drawn inspiration, and which had been the base of nearly all his work up to NOCES and RENARD (1917).

Nevertheless the author of the OCTUOR and of so many other compositions into which there enters not one ounce of Russian material (Russian, that is, in the sense that Rimsky's SADKO is Russian) evidently considers himself, even today, an essentially national artist. Before deciding whether this pretension is justified, we must try to solve a question of more general order: How can we determine the *national* character of any musical composition?

In other words: wnat criterion can we employ to discover whether a given composer is national, and whether another given composer is not? . . .

Are we to call a work "national" when it conforms to the musical traditions of the country, or not merely to the musical traditions, but to the country's modes of thinking and feeling, and to its conception of art? . . . Admitting that each nation has what you might call its genius, something peculiar to it, and manifest particularly in its musical feeling, and even in its very conception of the sonorous art, and of musical beauty, how are we to compute the specific characteristics of this "genius"? . . . France, certainly, possesses its musical traditions; we know them from the compositions of the masters, which seem to display among themselves a certain consanguinity, but this is very indefinite and undefinable. And who moreover guarantees us against the insurgence of some great composer who will turn the lot of these traditions bottom side up? One may be sure that in such a contingency, people will not fail to object to this "new movement," and against this "revolutionary" stuff they will set the "true French tradition"; but . . . since the musician of genius will, in spite of all this, impose himself . . . they will end by annexing him, and by discovering that although he innovates, it is "nevertheless undeniable that he" connects with the above mentioned "tradition" and that he is only developing it, and enriching it. Such, in short, was the story of Debussy, at first rejected as "against clear ideas," "contrary to the Latin genius," and so forth, and today (quite rightly) considered the *French* musician *par excellence* . . .

The desire to annex a man of genius is the expression not only of a very natural national pride, but also of the idea, or rather presentiment that a man of genius can't help being representative of a country, a nation, and that, in consequence, he *ought* to be connectable in one way or another with his precursors, who have reflected each in his way the spirit of their nation. In this sense one may say that genius has always a passport, that it can't help having one, even if it doesn't want to; thus reducing Stravinsky's remark to a demand that the artist ought to have genius; or that denying an artist national character one denies his talent; and that to say a given artist has talent and no national character is to emit an antinomy . . .

We should try to discover Stravinsky's passport. It will not be easy; for if it is undeniable that the man of genius is necessarily, in one sense, "traditionalist," his very function consists in realizing and bringing to light certain facets of the national

35

spirit which have, up to his day, remained hidden, which have existed perhaps only as latent potential, and which have seemed perhaps wholly alien to that spirit. In Stravinsky's case the element of innovation is particularly noticeable; to such a degree that many, even among his admirers, deny that there is any national character to his work subsequent to PULCINELLA. This seems to me a prize example of that disastrous method which works not from historic facts — here the series of extant musical compositions of the Russians — but with general ideas, such as "the Slavic soul" or "the Latin genius," and so forth; ideas which aren't even the product of an *abstraction* but merely a sort of residuum, the lees of divers impressions and images. If we want to find Stravinsky's passport we should keep free of these vague conglomerations, and keep hold of the relations which exist — ought to exist — between his art and the actual works of his predecessors, remaining where possible in the domain of fact . . .

The beginning of Russian music is usually dated from Glinka, and rightly . . .

Glinka's music differs from that of his predecessors and contemporaries in the very nature of melodies chosen, and also in the method of treatment.

The Russian musical folk-lore was a true *terra incognita* at the beginning of the last century. The dilettantes, and naturally even more the foreigners, knew nothing of Russian songs but the semi-popular stuff that had already felt the influence of to the Russians, and who gave it nationalization papers in our policed and learned music; but ROUSSLANN and LUDMILA is based on the *contrast* between the Russian world and the Asiatic . . . Ultimately one finds this contrast even in the OISEAU DE FEU, the only work in which Stravinsky has offered sacrifice to musical orientalism. Everywhere and always, in Russian music since Glinka, the Orient is treated as a picturesque element, its characteristics serve to underline still more heavily the specific characteristics of Russian song . . . Such a success as the LIFE FOR THE CZAR, in which Mozart, Italian opera, the French *opera comique,* and Russian song are composed into a living unity, bears witness to the profound affinity existing between Russian musical sensibility and European musical culture . . . Stravinsky's case seemed incomprehensible, and the author of the SYMPHONY FOR WIND INSTRUMENTS seemed devoid of national character to those (still the immense majority) who repeat the old gag about Scratch the Russian you find the Tartar. They think Russian art ought, and of necessity, to be violent, bedizened, nostalgic . . . But any one knowing the good period of Russian history, its golden age, from the reign of Alexander 1st through the first years of Nicholas 1st will grasp the true filiation of Stravinsky. This period gives us Glinka, the first of the Russian composers, and also Pushkin, the greatest poet of Russia, whom even Dostoevsky proclaimed the "very incarnation of Russian genius." Pushkin, like Glinka, owes much to occidental masters, he was fed on foreign writing, especially French and

English, both Chenier and Byron exercising immense influence on him.

I cite only these two cases, but one might cite many others, works impregnated with this taste, this measure, this equilibrium, or even marked with the classic spirit, qualities, that is, which the West is wont to claim as its own particular property.

These qualities appear likewise in the architecture of Alexander the First, "Empire" triumphing in Petersburg, differing wholly from ancient Moscow, where Italian barocco mingles with forms taken from Asia. If we go back still further, beyond the Mongol invasions that modified the visage of antique Russia, we will find the same care for a harmony, the same formalist research, the same so called "classic" spirit, in both the Russian painting and building, that had drunk in Byzantine traditions, which being Byzantine were, in consequence, hellenistic; these were absorbed, and created admirable works, greatly superior to the debased orientalistic product of the Muscovite era . . .

If occidental traditions had been really alien to Russian mentality and sensibility, the churches of Pskov and Novgorod, their frescoes, their ikons; and later in Petersburg under Alexander 1st, the apparition of artists like Glinka and Pushkin, or today a work like Stravinsky's OEDIPE, that is to say all this art of equilibrium, and luminosity, truly Apollonian, would be absolutely inexplicable. It is perfectly explainable if one admits that the Russians are not aliens to the family of occidental races, bred on Graeco-Roman tradition; and that these artists, going for their schooling to European culture find themselves in their normal habitat, and but take up something rightly their own . . .

When Stravinsky turns toward Bach or Handel, he follows *one* of the Russian traditions, and presents one of the numerous facets of Russia, the same one that Glinka presents in turning to Mozart, or Pushkin when he follows Moliere or Tirso de Molina's GUEST OF STONE; or Tschaikovsky with his flagrant Italianisms, Rimsky and Balakireff studying Berlioz and Liszt, or Scriabine following Wagnerian fashions. If Stravinsky declares that the last of these has no passport, it merely means that he denies the musical value of his work; having for it an almost physical repulsion he fails to perceive its Russian filiation, its affinity with Tschaikovsky, who emerges directly from Glinka, the common ancestor of them all.

This historic excursion should help us to understand the situation of the various musical groups and parties at the moment of Stravinsky's *debut*. Stravinsky studied in Petersburg, under Rimsky's direction. Nevertheless his first compositions, SYMPHONIE IN E-FLAT 1905-7, FAUN AND SHEPHERDESS, a suite for voice and orchestra 1907, SCHERZO FANTASTIQUE 1908, and various melodies for voice and piano 1908, '10, '11, show scarcely any trace of the Five, whose influence is only later apparent. His first works conform rather to the aesthetic of the Petersburg *conservatoire*.

40

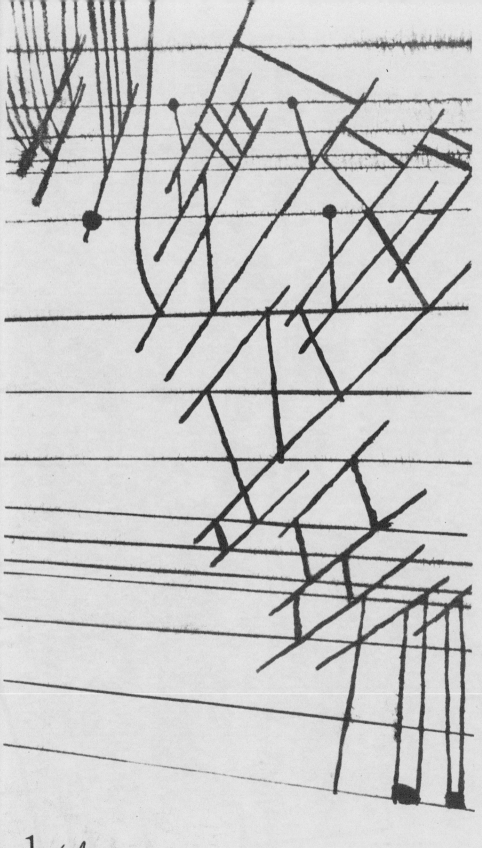

Founded by Anton Rubinstein, this conservatory was from its inception the stronghold of academism . . . This neuter style that reduces the works of the masters into formula — this being the very essence of academism — still exercises a great influence on the younger Russian composers, who regard it both as "classicism" and as "romanticism" (the latter term being void of meaning) . . .

The young Stravinsky passed through this also. And the fact would seem highly significant, if one considers the path later taken by our composer. It seems as if, after a long *detour*, Stravinsky in his latest works has come back to, or rediscovered certain conceptions which were perhaps already ripening in his mind at the start, but which he was incapable of realizing at that time, even if he were then conscious of them . . . For the moment I wish merely to indicate that if one will notice the earliest works of Stravinsky and the eclecticism of his start, one will better understand what he is now getting at with his classicism . . .

One might say that academism has no party, it is a language *par excellence* cosmopolite, and attains, in art, the ideal held up by Esperanto. Nothing is more like one conservatory than . . . another conservatory.

Thus the first works of Stravinsky belong to no national tradition — unless one considers academism itself a tradition, although it has rather the nature of a ubiquitous malady. Our composer takes contact with his native land, first in the FIRE BIRD, breaking there with eclecticism never thereto to return . . .

41

What marks this ballet as national is not, as I see it, the popular turn of melodies treated by the composer, but the filiation, that is to say the FIRE BIRD, connects directly with the picturesque, descriptive, decorative style of Rimsky-Korsakov particularly with the COQ D'OR and KASTCHEI THE IMMORTAL . . . After this honorific wreath offered to his teacher, Stravinsky gives up Rimsky and his friends once and for all. The only one of the Five with whom he will still from time to time take contact, is Moussorgsky. The relations between the author of BORIS, and the author of NOCES are fairly complex and have never yet, so far as I know, been analyzed . . .

Immediately after the FIRE BIRD the composer takes quite a new path, he commits the revolutionary act in the sense that he introduces into Russian music, conceptions and a style which had been up till that moment absolutely foreign to it. Stravinsky's evolution surprises us usually by its brusque turns, the sudden leaps, which seem to the spectator like so many breaks with the past; but never has the dissolution of continuity been so complete as between the FIRE BIRD and PETROU-SCHKA. One may easily go wrong at this point, for the melodic matter treated by the composer seems to establish a sort of connecting link between the "Russian" works of Stravinsky and those of his immediate predecessors. But one cannot too often repeat that: in art it is the way a thing is made to function that counts. From PETROUSCHKA onward this way differs fundamentally from the procedures of Rimsky-Korsakov, Borodine, and Balakireff.

In trying to trace the national origins of Stravinsky's art the principal difficulty is not offered by OEDIPE, but by PETROUSCHKA. To judge how greatly this ballet of Stravinsky's, and the works of his that follow it, differ from those of the Five, one need but compare the Fair scene in Rimsky's THE WORD OF THE CITY OF KITEGE with the first scene of PETROUSCHKA. We will analyze that difference later. For the moment suffice it to note clearly that Russian life, speaking in a general way: rites, games, beliefs, customs, costumes, special modes of thought and sensation, is and are musically realized by Stravinsky in an absolutely new and original fashion . . .

I have tried to prove that Stravinsky's "Europeanism" doesn't prevent his being profoundly national; a Russian in being "occidental" merely obeys one of the basic traditions of his race, and of his country. But looking closely, we find that the role of the composer of the SACRE in occidental musical life is very different from that which his Russian predecessors had to be content with . . . Stravinsky's position is quite different; he is a creator of European forms, taking "form" in its largest sense . . .

Stravinsky has assimilated European musical culture, he is penetrated with its laws, with its traditions. If he modifies them, if he imposes a new orientation, he innovates not as a foreigner introducing new ideas and new procedures, but as an autochthonous entity, modifying the spirit of his *milieu* from within. This revolutionary is the child of the land where he works, where he creates, transforming musical conceptions which belong both to it and to him. The new style which he introduces in Europe is by no means a product or "function" of the matter that he has treated for a decade — i.e., Russian song. Neither the polyphony of Stravinsky's art, nor its tonal structure, nor its harmonic complexity, nor its syncopated rhythms have come from Russia: all these characteristics mark the conclusion and the renewal of certain purely occidental traditions.

The Russian Stravinsky, author of the SACRE and of OEDIPE is the most European, the most essentially occidental of all extant musicians, if these terms "European" and "occidental" signify a certain type of artistic culture . . .

One of the characteristics of our epoch is the almost exaggerated development of national schools in music, each trying to affirm its own complete independence. It would be a delusion to swallow the idea that this exacerbated particularism can be surmounted by the creation of a cosmopolitan idiom in which all the differences would be mutually compensated and neutralized. It would scarcely be desirable, and it would be in any case beyond possibility. If Stravinsky has a place above these differences, if he seems to us today the most notable representative of the European spirit in music, it is, not because he is international, but, contrarily, because he is essentially national. His universality comes from his genius, or paraphrasing his own formula: the passport takes him over the frontiers . . .

Critics of Stravinsky's technique tend ordinarily to consider his art in a lump, neglecting the differences between one period

44

of it, and another, although these differences are quite worthy of note.

The critic, inclined to exaggerate the technical characteristics of the opus or period that he considers particularly significant, tries to find these characteristics constantly and all over the shop. Thus, for the majority of musicians Stravinsky's typical procedures are those of the SACRE, or, for another group, the very different ones of the OCTUOR. And thence, from the angle of these procedures, they consider the means used by Stravinsky in all the rest of his work, finding them in germ in such works as precede the work considered as typical, and following their development in the subsequent products . . . For me, the characteristic of Stravinsky's evolution is, precisely, its discontinuity; there is lack of what one can properly call progressive development from one work to another, but each one of the works (the important ones) suffices, in a certain sense, to itself, and should, in consequence, be examined separately and not as a function of some other which it is said to prepare or complete . . .

It seems to me none the less true that if we wish to understand one of these works we must set aside all idea of progress and that we definitely must not consider it as a section of a long unbroken chain stretching from the FIRE BIRD to APOLLO.

There are composers who have aspired their life long to a single goal, who have always wished to accomplish one sole work, and their compositions, often abundant, have been simply

45

a series of reaches and endeavours toward the unique thing, which has remained always a dream, but a dream that has functioned i. e., has sustained and guided the artist in his endeavour. This is not the case with Stravinsky. He has always set himself a precise goal, a concrete thing to be done, and he has accomplished what he set out to do, by means and procedures specially chosen for the effect, and which have given place, at opportune moment, to other means exactly suited to the new problem he set himself.

But if on the one hand, Stravinsky's technique, his melodic, harmonic, and rhythmic writing, his instrumental procedures are conditioned by the aim set, by the problem there to be solved, it is certain, on the other hand, that this problem itself has depended on the means then at the composer's disposal. If Stravinsky has set himself such and such a problem in place of some other; if he has wished to do precisely this thing and not another, that has depended on his technical equipment, of the means at his disposal at that particular moment. There is intimate proportion between the means and the end; and that explains the composer's successes, the absence of flat failures in his career, he has always done what he wished because he has always wished to do what he could do, and what would realize his own possibilities . . . He himself grows, indubitably he develops, but each stage of his musical life corresponds to one or several works, quite complete in their kind, and in which one might say there was no gap between intention and realization.

There is very little originality, from the technical side, in the FIRE BIRD, whatever its first auditors may have thought in 1908, especially here in France where the last works of Rimsky-Korsakov, KASTCHEI THE IMMORTAL, LE COQ D'OR were then very little known . . .

If the general conception of the FIRE BIRD is closely attached to the "Russian Story" style, determined by Rimsky, and in which Russian and Oriental melodies are woven into an harmonic idiom close to Wagner's, there is also generous use of Debussyian and Scriabinian methods; linkings of ninths, elevenths, and thirteenths diversely altered, augmented fifths, whole tone scales, parallel progressions, etc. . . .

One can find no elements in this work "more definitely Stravinskian" and "whose significance shall be revealed later only" than those offered in Rimsky's infernal dance of KASTCHEI's subjects, with its obstinately hammered rhythm and in the character of its tonal planes, generally very marked, unequivocal, despite the chromatisms and the whole tone scales which submerge them. Note that the solidity and definiteness of the tonal planes are certainly among the most characteristic traits of Stravinsky's harmonic language . . .

We must now stop for a moment, seeing that the FIRE BIRD, in regard to instrumentation marks a critical stage in the orchestral work of Stravinsky; meaning that in this ballet the composer pushes to their ultimate limits the orchestral conceptions of his forerunners, against which conceptions PETROU-SCHKA showed already a decisive reaction, that was to be more

47

accentuated year by year, growing yearly more conscious, more systematic.

The instrumental conception reigning in the FIRE BIRD is that which dominates nearly all music of the XIXth, and of the opening years of the XXth century, the orchestra is considered as a vast, very complex apparatus, a sort of giant organ whose stops are constituted by the divers groups of instruments . . . Wagner orchestrated with harmonies. Nevertheless the instrumental procedures, even of those who rebelled, flowed back ultimately into the development of the initial drift: Wagner triumphed, Wagner whose orchestra came out of Weber's . . . All the masters of orchestra of the opening XXth century, with very rarest exception (Ravel for example, but only after the DAPHNIS) have, each in his own way, realized the same orchestral conception, obeying under different cloak or appearance a common tendency which I will call "the romantic" or "magical."

Stravinsky one day declared that Wagner's orchestra played the organ . . . But mightn't one say the same of the FIRE BIRD orchestra? Let us first understand the meaning of "faire orgue." When Stravinsky applies this expression to Wagner, he means that the latter systematically uses what one might call "orchestral pedal," which gives his instrumentation exactly the fat and compact quality so characteristic of it. To the eye many pages of Wagner appear as linear structure rather aerean, despite the richness of harmony, but in listening to the orchestra one finds that the author has plugged up all the holes, filled all the corners, making sure that the melodic lines are always projected over a continuous sonorous foundation. In this regard the orchestra of Rimsky, Debussy, and of Stravinsky in the FIRE BIRD, differs completely from Wagner's; they employ orchestral pedal only spasmodically; their instrumentation is ventilated, the orchestral web (literally woof, *trame*) is become tenuous, transparent, not fearing even discontinuity. One no longer seeks the mixture of timbres so much as their opposition, and one is thus brought to underline the specific characters of the different orchestral timbres, and to allot the different groups of instruments their own individuality — abolished by Wagnerian aesthetic, which had tended to the "molten" . . .

From this instrumental aesthetic, sprung evidently from TRISTAN which, desiring that nothing shall pierce, or jut out, ends up in a species of orchestral camouflage, to the all quite angular, all faceted orchestra of the FIRE BIRD (considering particularly the first tableau) the distance is, assuredly, great . . . Historically the orchestra was created by joining one instrumental group to another; but in our modern conception, it appears as a generative apparatus for timbres, a vast keyboard of almost unlimited possibilities; it is no longer a grouping together, a product of the addition of different instruments as it was in the pre-Beethoven period. From this point of view Stravinsky's orchestra before PETROUSCHKA "plays the organ" quite as much as Wagner's, the author of the FIRE BIRD merely

49

uses his organ differently from the author of TRISTAN . . .

It is a common affair today, because a century has passed since the divorce of the very structure of a work from its realization on the orchestral plane; and this divorce could only occur, little by little, because one had got used to thinking of the orchestra as a generative apparatus for timbres . . .

It is probably with Weber that the orchestra first pretended to impose its own worth and is revealed as a powerful means of action, a sort of magic, a transfixing the wax image, (envoutement) bewitchment, acting directly on the sensibility without an intellectual registering. The charm of the Mozartian orchestra is, in addition, inseparable from the development of ideas, a development that demands a certain effort of attention on our part, a sort of tenseness of spirit almost nil for those who know the piece already, while Weber's orchestra, and still more the orchestra of Wagner, Berlioz, Rimsky-Korsakov, Debussy, or Stravinsky, before PETROUSCHKA, sends us into a quasi-hypnotic state. I have called it "magic" orchestra, for one of the effects of any magic action is that it tends to plunge the subject into a receptive, into an exclusively passive, state . . .

The FIRE BIRD is the very type of this art of bewitchment. If we can even now become aware, and understand that this timbre-factory, the modern orchestra is by no means an ineluctable necessity, it is to Stravinsky that we owe our enlightenment; for he first, in PETROUSCHKA broke with romantic instrumentation, and gave back its ancient role to the orchestra.

50

The orchestra of PETROUSCHKA marked the end of the reign of "beautiful sonorities," and even of strange, new, exotic sonorities, etc., and of these sonorous combinations which of themselves, detached, without relation to anything else, plunge us instantly into beatitude wholly physical. The instrumentation of this work is strictly subordinated to the melodic ideas; it does not exist save as function of these ideas, which it strives to set in relief, to realize as completely as possible, without pretending to impose itself by itself on the auditor. Thus one might say there are no more "orchestral effects" in PETROUSCHKA, for the combinations of timbres are determined by the development of the melodic, harmonic, and rhythmic ideas; and the value of these combinations only appears in their mutual relations, that is to say, in revealing the significance of the melodic phrases to which these combinations give body . . .

If in PETROUSCHKA the composer reestablishes the functional role of orchestra, and terminates the divorce between the melodic structure of a work and its instrumental realization, a divorce which dates back to Weber, one might suppose that having started on this path Stravinsky has ever since persisted therein, and that the SACRE, for example, marks a still further anabasis as compared to PETROUSCHKA. It doesn't. In the SACRE, the composer "plays the organ" again, his orchestra is no longer, as in PETROUSCHKA, linear and conditioned by the musical structure, he hunts out instrumental combinations for their own sake, he gives himself up to the play of timbres in the effort to create a special atmosphere of terror and mystery, as for example in the prelude to the second tableau. His orchestral technique is there adapted to the character of the work, to the precise end he had assigned himself. Whence the impression of black magic, the magic force of the SACRE, and the purely receptive state into which it sends us, thanks also to rhythmic texture.

One cannot too often repeat that it is only in developing the element of timbre in music, and in giving it a certain autonomy, that the composer can assume the role of enchanter (against which Nietzsche so violently protested) that is, manage to have us give ourselves over wholly to him hands tied, feet tied, our wills wholly abolished. For melody and harmony, if they are to be assimilated, if they are to touch us, or charm us, demand necessarily from us a certain intellectual operation, an act of synthesis . . .

The two conceptions face each other in LE ROSSIGNOL, that curious work which looks like a cross-roads in Stravinsky's compositions, a sort of cross-roads where he hesitates and falls back at sight of the divergent routes there before him . . . One observes the predominance of melodic idea, using timbre for its (the melodic) purpose . . .

Already in 1916, 1917, 1918, with RENARD, NOCES, HISTOIRE DU SOLDAT, he returned to the instrumental conceptions applied by him for the first time in PETROUSCHKA, now developing them by reducing the dimensions of his orchestra. This reduction is extremely significant; it is, indeed, the direct consequence of his drift toward treating the orchestra as an assembly in which each instrument or group executes its part in a polyphonic structure . . . At the limit of this system one finds, the quatuor, or in a more general way, chamber music. For what essentially differentiates chamber music from orchestra properly so called, is not only the number of instruments, but their modus of use . . . They are conditioned by the thematic development. The cymbalum itself, that Stravinsky uses so happily in RENARD, fills an harmonic function, which its special sonority serves to make clear.

The typical work of this instrumental method is the OCTUOR, a work almost wholly polyphonic. But Stravinsky remains equally faithful to the method in stage works, MAVRA, OEDIPUS, and APOLLO-MUSAGETES. These last two works are especially interesting from this angle, for side by side with contrapuntal pages are pages of harmonic writing in chordal structure that ought, it might seem, to tempt or shove the composer into playing with timbres. He does nothing of the sort, on the contrary we notice a determination to renounce all colour effects, to the point that he even refuses to underline certain particularly striking harmonic aggregates by instrumental groups thereto appropriate . . . The concourse of instruments has here no objective save their unfoldings, their contacts, their balancings. The orchestra wants to be forgotten, and succeeds in that aim.

But here, and let us not overlook it, the musician sets himself, as in the OEDIPUS, a precise goal; he adapts his orchestral procedures to the problem he has set himself to solve . . . The body of the orchestra, if we may so call it, seems to dematerialize in his later productions; a body that had been in the FIRE BIRD and the SACRE so unwontedly beautiful, plump and strong, now submitted to ascetic regime, reduced strictly to minimum, which allows the animating spirit to show through, and which shines only with the beauty of the "soul" of the music, alias melody . . .

As we have seen, the FIRE BIRD neither innovates by harmonic writing nor by instrumental procedures, it is quite of its epoch, but with PETROUSCHKA all changes brusquely.

The chromatism gives place to a diatonic style whereto Stravinsky remains still faithful, though with important modifications. With rare exceptions chromatism does not again appear in his work, save in the SACRE, in prelude and second tableau, with traces in PETROUSCHKA . . . The very concept of "chord" changes in PETROUSCHKA, for Stravinsky has abandoned the vertical harmonic writing that ruled in the FIRE BIRD, replacing it by an horizontal melodic style, that develops up to the polyphonics of his last compositions.

In the FIRE BIRD the polyphony is still rudimentary, consisting in nothing more than imitation harmonic in character, which now and again breaks a chord, but in PETROUSCHKA we find real combinations of melodies, and real contrapuntual

54

developments which are not determined by harmony, but on the contrary determine it by their own contacts . . . The tonality is always clearly affirmed. But it is precisely in PETROUSCHKA where no tonal ambiguity is possible that Stravinsky first employs certain procedures that might be termed polytonal . . . The SACRE offers us still more significant examples . . .

And yet I hardly think we can use the term polytonality in its true sense, when speaking of Igor Stravinsky . . . This does not occur in Stravinsky's work, either in the SACRE or in later compositions, in him there is always a fundamental tonality, rigorously affirmed, and to which the melodic lines, or harmonic complexes belonging to a different tonality are temporarily joined or referred, but the other tonality is finally abandoned, or melted through modulation into the fundamental tonality. Stravinsky, in brief, merely aggrandizes the use of passing notes, lying outside his tonality; in him one finds passing themes, melodies, and even whole phrases which take the role of harmonic retards and anticipations. But under the complexity of his harmonic weaving, or straddling of two, sometimes three tonalities, one makes out, always, the principal tonal plane, which in the end absorbs the others and proclaims itself in a cadence which wipes out all ambiguity . . .

The polyphony of the SACRE is much more developed than that of PETROUSCHKA . . . In this respect, as well as in respect to its orchestration the SACRE is much less "new" than

PETROUSCHKA, and even marks a sort of retrogression from it, and toward conceptions which the author is later definitely to abandon.

And yet the SACRE, at its first appearance revolutionized its auditors; people thought it upset the whole of music. And even today it appears as the most audacious, most formidable work by Stravinsky, the one that marks the debut of a new musical era and definitely breaks with the past. But the more often one hears the SACRE, the more one studies its score, the more clearly one perceives the fundamental error of this opinion concerning it. A very comprehensible error, all of us have committed it. What caused it is the power, the really unheard of power and complexity of rhythmic life animating its pages; and added thereto the violence, the splendour of orchestration, and finally the systematic use of harmonic aggregations, and of melodic phrases alien to the fundamental tonality, that is, the pseudo-polytonality of which we have spoken which violently wounded our ears, but made them taste also the bitter, painful delectations . . .

The SACRE, if one set aside its undeniable aesthetic value, is one of the most characteristic productions of Stravinsky, but it is also the one that has been the most dangerous to him, and everything he has written since 1914 is in profound reaction against it. If Stravinsky's art exists today, if this admirable genius is what he now is, if modern music is oriented in the ways wherein we now observe it, it is only because this composer, assuredly not without difficulty, not without

56

terrible efforts, and grievous sacrifices, has renounced the SACRE, renounced its pomps and its seductions, for this splendid creation is in a certain respect not a beginning, but an end and a conclusion . . .

In deliberately renouncing combinations of autonomous timbres, after the SACRE, Stravinsky was, naturally, drawn to abandon simultaneously the vertical writing which ruled that epoch and to which he had made in the SACRE, ample oblation . . . After that it is melody alone that reigns in the work of Stravinsky . . .

It is the song, the MELOS, which becomes the soul of Stravinsky's music, and not only the soul but the body, for all the other elements, timbres, harmony, rhythms, as we shall soon see, obey it and end by being integrated, drawn into it. The real meaning of the revolution accomplished by Stravinsky is revealed not by the SACRE, but by the THREE PIECES FOR CLARINETTE (1920) which are both a program and a profession of faith . . . It is after NOCES especially and the HISTOIRE DU SOLDAT, that the "vocal" character comes into Stravinsky's art . . . Song, the melody was at the beginning of music, and the art of sound, one might say, returns to its fount and origin . . .

The rhythmic element is usually considered the preponderant and particularly characteristic one in Stravinsky, the rhythm, its variety, complexity, vigour seem to determine his style, giving it the turn and colour which make it instantly recognizable. One cannot deny the importance of the element which gives ground for considering the author of NOCES the most gifted creator of rhythms who has ever existed, but I think that the development of rhythm in his work is the functioning product of his harmonic and melodic development, and that the rhythmic peculiarities of Stravinsky's style, as likewise his tonal and polyphonic writing, are conditioned by his general conception of music. If he has enriched the rhythmic domain; if he has given a new drive to our imagination; to our rhythmic sensibility, and thereby raised up a veritable musical revolution, this coheres with his having attained the creation of a new sonorous language — tonal and melodic . . .

The field of rhythmic combinations is, indeed, limitless, but one isn't free in it, any more than in the domain of harmonic combinations. One must orientate, trace paths, the choice is not easy to make operant, mere arbitrariness is no more permissible here than anywhere else in music.

From PETROUSCHKA onward one sees Stravinsky putting to proof the rhythmic virtuosity which causes his reputation . . . The SACRE marks the beginning of his rhythmic invention. The composer really creates new metres, and displays an inexhaustible rhythmic fecundity in the HISTOIRE DU SOLDAT, RENARD, NOCES, the SYMPHONIES FOR WIND INSTRUMENTS, and the OCTUOR . . .

One must concede that there is rhythmic structure only where there is melodic and polyphonic development over a tonal basis, whatever it may be. Purely harmonic and atonal music is always rhythmically amorphous . . . It is only then that the rhythmic formula takes on the character of necessity, of logic, and imposes itself upon us as objective reality *(neces-site)*, and not merely as an arbitrary construction which happens to be as it is, but might as well be something other. It is precisely this objective reality that Stravinsky has constantly sought, and he has attained it only when he could integrate rhythm in melody — which is what I am driving at.

Thus the identity which is so often claimed for the rhythmic forms of negro music with those of Stravinsky, appears to me wholly false. Assuredly the Russian composer was affectable by the seductions of Negro-American orchestras . . .

What I want to designate as Stravinsky's "melodic" rhythm is something very different from rhythm *"pure,"* from the *"rhythm in itself"* of primitive peoples. There is rhythmic primitivism in Stravinsky, as there is the harmonic primitivism of which I have spoken — and they both appear, in analysis, as very refined forms of art . . .

Despite transient influences undergone, the rhythmic forms of Stravinsky are the product of our occidental musical evolution; they develop in realizing European metric concepts; they have become embodied thanks only to the fruitful convention of the bar . . .

Folk dreamed of "rhythmic liberty," and the only means "imaginable" of attaining it was the suppression of measured bars (even bars). But for a long time people have said: Liberty is sterile in art.

Nothing is fecund save the strife versus the obstacle, there is no creation save in the action of overcoming resistance . . . Stravinsky has never destroyed the measured bar; he struggles against it, he disarticulates it, he multiplies and hooks up the different metres, but he never permits himself once, and for good and all, to get rid of this bothersome fiction, for he needs the annoyance, the resistance, against which to leap and surge, for there is no rhythmic diversity without stability . . .

In OEDIPUS Stravinsky renounces not only the stratification of metres, but even the measured bar as something to break away from; he conforms with docility to its strong and weak accents without even syncopation, the diversities of melodic accents, their surprising variants give place to forms stable and four-square, in unmodified repetition, as in the airs of CREON and TIRESIAS. Save for a few passages, the chorals show a like simplicity, rhythmic stability and uniformity seeming in absolute contradiction to the tendencies of Stravinskian art as we understand them. But do we so well understand them? A little more and we should find ourselves crying "treason," for an artist is not allowed to disappoint the general expectation and to break our effigy of him. Obviously he means not to adapt himself to his audience and re-do SACRE and NOCES to meet its demand. In which case he'd be blamed anyway, for repeating himself, so that it is up to us to adapt ourselves: to try to understand and even to modify our ideas about him — evidently wrong ideas. Could anything show this more peremptorily than APOLLO MUSAGETES, with its simple dance formulae? No unex-

60

pected accent breaks in to modify the line of melody, developing perfectly at its ease in the frame of a measure uniformly "normal" . . .

The latest compositions would appear to be toward reestablishing the exclusive domination of melodic thought.

The same is discoverable in his writing for voice . . .

The popular poems he uses, the texts he writes in popular speech have one trait in common, their illogicality . . . Save in such exceptions as CHANT DISSIDENT the words are put together not according to their meaning but because of sonorous affinities, or far-fetched association of images . . .

In treating a text the musician may do various things: try to amplify the emotional condition expressed in the words; try to translate the words one by one, commentating, describing the images. Or as Moussorgsky did, or thought he was doing; one may follow all the inflections of the spoken phrase, underlining them, bringing out the music latent in the speech; or else one may more or less adapt to the text a melody inspired by the text but having its own musical significance.

The relations of word and musical sound are quite different in Stravinsky. His songs have a peculiarity, the words have the same role as rhythmic accents, melodies, harmonies, that is, the same role as the musical elements . . . The line of articulate sounds is combined in melodic line even more strictly than one instrument joins another in orchestra, with this difference also, that in his songs the two sonorous lines are presented by a single executant. But neither element has a value if isolated; only the product of their fusion — articulate sounds in melodic current — has a musical signification . . .

I have pointed out that in later years his music was vocal in character, even his polyphony showing choral conception; this essentially "singing" character is not found in the songs we have just been discussing. Stravinsky seems to care nothing whatever for the real nature of the human voice, or for its possibilities; he treats it as an instrument; the melodic phrase is often given to the accompanying instruments, while the voice intervenes as harmonic component, or traces arabesques which find their take-off in the articulate sounds, and in the verbal accents, with which the composer takes utmost liberty. CHANT DISSIDENT in the FOUR RUSSIAN SONGS, shows a tendency toward melodic vocal style . . .

In NOCES, the chief choral work, this instrumental writing disappears altogether, the articulate sounds continue to serve as musical elements (their logical sense insignificant) they underline the rhythmic accents of the vocal phrase, but this latter acquires a personality and a definite significance, the instruments being reduced to the role of accompaniment . . .

Some of his texts are of popular creation, as in NOCES, some his own, and in them examination would show that he takes the greatest liberties with the popular style, mixing dialects and epochs with no regard to historic verisimilitude or philology. The characters' language in NOCES is hybrid, monstrous, belonging to no fixed epoch, never spoken anywhere or any when in Russia, all of which faked archaism simply doesn't matter, he enlivens, distorts, changes the pronunciation or accent, because he is using them as musical raw matter, caring for nothing but the sonority which serves as bones in his melody. Which is, is it not, the principle governing all great vocal compositions of the XVIIIth, and even of part of the XIXth century? Have not authors of operas, airs for oratorio, ensembles and parts of chorals done the same? . . .

Faced with a text inspired by Pushkin (MAVRA) or a libretto in Mediaeval Latin (OEDIPUS REX), Stravinsky behaves very much as with a folk or pseudo-folk song or story, i. e., as a vocal composer who cares only for the sounds, the musical feeling and the characteristics of the human voice . . . One thus discerns a formalist tendency in the evolution of his song-writing in the degree that the human voice is detached from the instrumental agglomerate; in the degree that its dominant melodic role is defined, that the orchestra is limited to accompanying it, the composer presses an artificial mould on his vocal phrase, he organizes it according to ancient conventions, thus giving it impersonality, a plastic beauty rather abstract.

I think one could write an entire volume on the forms in Stravinsky's art, so great is the diversity of procedures in his already long career.

Stravinsky has written a great deal for the theatre. He is

even, in limited sense, a dramatist. But his operas, his ballets, are constructed as works of pure music, that is to say their development is submitted to no extra-musical rule, it is in no way conditioned by scenic action, poetic image, or by any abstract idea . . .

The unity of the SACRE is obtained not by symmetric structure and the return of one or several fundamental themes, but by perfect homogeneity of a clearly characterized melodic, harmonic, and rhythmic style. Each of the 11 episodes has one or two motifs of its very own, melodies or rhythmic formulae diversely treated with repetitions, rhythmic and harmonic variations, contrapuntal development . . .

What we may call this "cellular structure," an assemblage of short episodes each having a characteristic melodic, rhythmic, and harmonic element, appears again in RENARD and in NOCES. But while the unity of the SACRE is obtained only by homogeneity of style, RENARD and NOCES have thematic unity and a symmetrical and, as you might say, "closed" composition: the end takes up the beginning . . .

We observe slightly varied application of this same "formal" principle in APOLLO MUSAGETES, and in OEDIPUS; tight compartments, composed by the dances in the ballet; by the airs, in the cantata; the OEDIPUS contains moreover a choral part which provides a sort of continuous current; APOLLO is not unlike a suite in which the finale resumes the initial motif in peroration, almost as in NOCES. In MAVRA where something happens on the stage, the music seems to follow the text more closely, but the strictly melodic structure and the lucky convention of airs and ensembles, allow the composer to maintain the rights and independence of the "sonorous art."

In purely instrumental works Stravinsky's diversity of forms — the variations in the OCTUOR, the choral in SYMPHONIES FOR WIND, etc. — does not prevent our discovering a general character. Let us admit it is negative. There is no "development" in Beethoven's sense of the term, in Stravinsky's music . . .

Stravinsky's developments consist generally in: contrapuntal combinations of short motifs, which remain in themselves almost unchanged (NOCES), or in deploying a melodic phrase which begets a succession of others, in this latter case (in the piano sonata for example) the development is what might be called material rather than formal . . .

We have examined briefly the different technical procedures used by Stravinsky from the FIRE BIRD to APOLLO MUSAGETES, and tried to understand the general orientation of his evolution, or more precisely, of the slow development of his musical language. We must now try to make out the meaning of this, and of what might be called the spirit of his art, which "spirit" can only be discovered by going on as we have begun and trying to answer the only question posited in art, that is the "How?" If we know how a thing is made we know its secrets, we know what the artist wanted to say, we reach the substance, the content via the form — which is really an impossibility for we only work with successive approximations, as does a geometer. Form and content are relative in the sense — too often forgotten — that whatsoever element we examine is both form and content; form in relation to one element, content in relation to another . . . The style is the first problem before us. I doubt whether the style is the man. But the style is the artist only up to a certain point . . .

I have already shown that Stravinsky's style is very different from that of his predecessors, and that his later abandonment of folk-lore for an international language and for something nearer to Bach by no means indicates that he became the less Russian or national. It is nevertheless true that his systematic use of popular themes gives his idiom, during that long period, a particular character comparable to that of the so-called "Russian" school, a character no longer audible in work done later than 1917.

But one must discriminate between PETROUSCHKA on one hand, and the SACRE, RENARD, and NOCES. Most of the themes in PETROUSCHKA are not of village, peasant, or fundamentally Russian origin; it is music of townsfolk already touched by occidental musical culture . . . There results a strange, but homogeneous and organic compost of waltzes, polkas, hand-organ music, Russian dances, and Tzigane ballads, sung by strolling artists . . . The melodies of PETROUSCHKA do not really belong to the composer, but he has taken this matter that was everybody's matter, and made it his own, organizing it in his own special ways.

The SACRE is of totally different inspiration. Some of its themes are taken from north Russian folk-lore wherein the ancient Russian traditions are better preserved. Others belong to the composer . . . Certain motifs in the SACRE show nothing specifically Russian, but all have certain qualities in common; diatonism, rhythmic accentuation, clarity of melodic contour, harmonic hardness, which give them what seems to us a certain archaic turn . . .

In NOCES and RENARD the proportion of melodic invention is much greater. Folk-lore is no longer his guide, and the models it offers him are so deformed and transposed as to be wholly unrecognizable . . .

Stravinsky's diatonic writing, the diversity, the freedom of rhythmic accents, his powerful dynamism are perfectly suited to the nature of the songs and dances of the Russian folk. The popular Russian music is in fact diatonic, while the songs of oriental people (Tartars) tend to chromatism; the augmented second beloved in oriental melody is very rare in purely Russian regions . . . The rhythm of Russian songs and dances is very complex, but the accentuation is always clear and rigorous. The rhythmic structure of oriental songs is characterized by lack of accentuation, by a sort of rhythmic softness and flexibility, allied with the abundance of vocalizations and ornaments . . . Nothing save rhythmic accentuation offers us the chance of perceiving time directly; oriental music frees us from the sensation of time; it places us, as one might say, outside duration, and pours out a sort of beatitude and peculiar inebriety for the auditor; making us lose notion of time . . . Russian song, on the contrary, exists in time, the precision and diversity of its rhythms hold the auditor in the realm of duration, it excites his activity, suggesting the sensations of movement, of development. Russian popular music is essentially dynamic . . . Stravinsky's procedures emphasize this dynamic character even more, and one might even say that his music is *"plus russe que nature"* . . .

If his Russian style seems to us truer and more direct than that of the Five, it is because he breaks with the habitual, and frees us from certain fashions too well known, but he replaces them by others; furnished by the sonorous art of the occident, as had been those of his predecessors.

Popular Russian song is, indeed modal. I have already insisted on the particularly tonal character of Stravinsky's writing, which tends regularly to reduce popular melody to occidental major-minor formulae . . . There is moreover the syncopy that Stravinsky so much uses. This appears very rarely in Russian popular music, and this break of metric equilibrium is not the least in its nature. The development of this process in Stravinsky's art is contrary to the spirit of Russian national music. He has introduced it as an element of alien origin, yet by grace of it, has managed to bring into value the metric variety and dynamism of popular song and dance . . . It is not a question, today, of restoring Russian popular music in complete purity, and creating a new musical culture on that basis; that would be an unrealizable, and also useless, endeavour. But one must underline the fact that the "Russian style" of Stravinsky's music is a mixed style, Russo-European . . .

By comparison with Moussorgsky, Stravinsky looks like a stylizer; thanks to the use of certain procedures he, as you might say, forces the note, he evokes a Russian much more brutal, uncouth, archaic than it has ever been in reality. And the most curious point is that he achieves this result in deforming Russian song by means furnished him by a refined musical culture, and a perfect acquaintance with European art.

Nevertheless Moussorgsky and Stravinsky appear to foreigners as the most authentic Russian composers, as the two who give the truest and least conventional image of Russia; we see that their routes are divergent, their attitudes to Russian song, are opposed. One regards reality as a mere material, and attains aesthetic verity directly; the other attains this same verity, and beauty, by rigorous observation and by a reproduction which he wishes, and believes to be absolutely faithful to the reality . . .

The subject of L'HISTOIRE DU SOLDAT, text by C. F. Ramuz, is still Russian, though the story belongs to an international cycle. Stravinsky's music for it, however, offers no longer anything specifically Russian save a few dance rhythms, and melodic inflections. He imposes on himself, for the first time, certain fixed forms elaborated by European musical culture, and keeps strictly within their frame, thus for the HISTOIRE DU SOLDAT he provides a short march, a little concerto, and the dances; a waltz, and a tango keeping the conventional outline.

In 1919 he visits Italy and unearths a Pergolesi dance-suite, which he orchestrates, modifies slightly, introducing some piquant harmonies, and this results in the exquisite PULCINELLA, a great success, but one which people regard as merely a clever pastiche, the amusement of a tired musician. Quite wrongly — for this work marks an important date in Stravinsky's career, I would even go so far as to say a date in modern musical history, for we here come upon a strange metamorphosis in our composer's method, his art takes on an extraordinary power and radiance. Before PULCINELLA he was very little followed or even imitated . . . Stravinsky's art seemed so personal and peculiar and so "Russian," that the occidentals were incapable of getting anything from it, unless, that is, they were content with obvious and too dangerous imitation. There is a complete change in this situation after PULCINELLA, and he becomes a deep and fruitful influence. His style has been freed from its "particularism"; as composer of this work, of the OCTUOR, and the PIANO CONCERTO he appears as an essentially European master. We have already affirmed that he always was European and that he is, still and always, Russian.

It was not the procedures but the style that changed in 1919. I insist on the distinction . . .

70

MAVRA, the OCTUOR, the CONCERTO, the PIANO SONATA, OEDIPUS, APOLLO are "type-works." I mean that for them the composer takes a certain form, that of the opera for example, or the concerto, or the ballet . . . Stravinsky adopts them entirely, *and* makes them his own. He creates inside this frame, adapting his procedures to it, bending his harmonic and melodic and rhythmic writing to it, and yet preserving his own character in them all . . . When Stravinsky composes a PIANO CONCERTO he adopts the scheme of this sort of work, introduces a somewhat Lisztian cadenza and writes, as is suitable, a work of virtuosity, which is, however, Stravinskian . . .

It seems extraordinary that the composer, so deliberately limiting himself in the smallest details, is able to preserve such great liberty both in the choice of melodies and in the manner of treating them, and that despite the disparity of elements used, he melts them into so perfect a unity . . .

And yet it all hangs together, and all these works show the hand of Stravinsky as definitely as do PETROUSCHKA, NOCES, and the SACRE. In every case he attains his unity, firstly by means of the strict frame imposed on the elements, by means of the cohesive force of the very forms themselves, treated by him with the so prodigious virtuosity, and thus showing themselves, despite their antiquity, extraordinarily fecund in the hands of a musician of genius and a great master of art; and thanks, finally, to his adopting in each work a certain group of procedures of writing, a certain technical language, which he maintains faithfully throughout the whole of the work,

71

so that it acquires a complete personality, and a "soul" of its own . . . But when one has established this relation (stupefying as it would have been for the first hearers of the SACRE to see the two names joined) I think one will find that the parentage is not with what is peculiar and individual in Bach, but with precisely what makes him so typical of his era. If Stravinsky has turned to the great Cantor, it is because he has discerned him as the master of continuous style, the musician above all others who has so perfected that development of musical thought which might be termed "dialectic," in which one (musical) idea begets another with such spontaneity and directness, without intervention of any psychological factor. It is not the religious work, or, more generally speaking, the vocal part of Bach that has affected Stravinsky, but exclusively the instrumental work in which this special construction is manifest . . .

From Bach he turns to Handel or Lully, but always to the past. So that his art seems baffling and incomprehensible to most of his auditors, even to those who admire and are ready to follow him. How, indeed, can this musician of genius who at first shocked, and then conquered us by his originality, dress himself in these old clothes, put on a mask, and try at all costs to be "banal," even if not always succeeding in being so? (though some people are fooled) . . .

We babble about the style of Debussy, Tchaikowsky, Pizzetti, but the *style* of a work is, speaking exactly, that where it is

2

impersonal, or rather, super-individual; it is that which is shared by several, that whereby a thing belongs to an epoch, or a country, or may even attain a universal meaning . . .

A style does not belong to an artist; he, as it were, bathes in a style, he finds it; he confers it on himself. His problem is to adapt it to himself, to make use of it in such a way that he manages by it to exteriorize his thought. There is *"manner"* which is a personal affair, which belongs really to the artist, which is the product of his reaction in face of *style,* and of individual assimilation of style by the creative imagination; and there is "style," as it were a collective product wherein certain modes of the age's or nation's thought, feeling, action, crystallize; this is true also for a group if it succeeds in imposing its spirit on the whole of a society.

It may seem that in the long run this is merely a quantitative difference; may not the group reduce itself to a single individual, a personality strong enough to impose his seal on the thought of his contemporaries? Manner and style merge? Can't what was at first an exclusively personal mode of thought, be imitated, and spread, and be transformed into style? These questions are particularly acute at this instant, for we, in our time, now that is, see just this imitation of certain details of writing, of certain procedures. But a "style" cannot be born in this way. It is the language which makes possible the birth of a work of art, which allows an artist to come out of himself, to address someone else and get into communication with him. If he does not find this collective language, which is not exterior to himself, but inside him, and which he, assuredly, modifies, he cannot create, or at least can create only by using the ersatz for style, a personal manner, which thanks to imitation has acquired a certain collective existence. He adapts this as best he may to his own needs. Nevertheless a style is never an obstacle for the creator, but on the contrary a powerful assistance; its caricature, the manner of one of his predecessors or his great contemporaries must always be overcome, surpassed, got rid of, if he would give exterior reality to what is in him . . .

The style carries the work, sustains it in the strife with time, and prevents its dying. What weakens, and bears the germ of decadence, is the ensemble of means used to bend the style to the personal needs of the author, his manner, his procedures, his tricks.

Don't try to twist this into meaning, or make me appear to mean that the more a work is neuter, the more it is void of personality, the greater its chance of survival; but this obligation of the artist to adapt a style to his own manner of feeling and thinking is a sad necessity; and the man of genius who should succeed in creating without submission to this, by reducing these individual elements to a minimum, would have nothing to fear from the future. For one can perfectly well conceive a great artist expressing himself totally in the language and forms of his time without modifying anything in them; and yet his work would remain personal,

74

and even unique if he carried the style of his time to a certain perfection.

Today this statement shocks us, it even sounds like a paradox, because style has been dead in music since the beginning of the 19th century; we have dealt since that date with nothing save forms of individual language which have each radiated more or less, and excited more or less imitation . . . In 19th-century work the cause of weakness, for imitation, and even development or adaptation of a certain *manner,* inhibits the creation of any new "typical" work *(oeuvre typique).* Thus the modern composer is always at strife with himself and this is much more dangerous than the strife he ought to wage against his environment, for he must at all cost hammer out a language of his own, since his epoch lacks a style, and if he doesn't elaborate a manner for himself he will assuredly fall into Wagnerism, or Debussyism, or Ravelism, or Stravinskyism.

Because he has felt, profoundly, the need of a style, of a super-individual framework, Stravinsky has turned to the XVIIIth-century masters . . . Is not the language resuscitated by Stravinsky the product of a mental structure very different from our own? Is the transposition of this style into the present anything more than a mere stylization, can it produce anything more than a pastiche?

The answer is that the OCTUOR, OEDIPUS, and APOLLO MUSA-GETES are very much alive . . .

If Stravinsky's effort is proved fecund, it is because the

XVIIIth-century forms of musical language possess a particular virtue (or inherent force) . . . and there is every reason for believing that we will have to return to them and to plunge ourselves into them *periodically,* even if it be merely for the purpose of following such plunge by producing something entirely different . . . They offer us the most undiluted example so far extant of what can be created by entirely autonomous musical thought, i. e., musical thought entirely governed by itself, drawing the whole matter out of its own particular deep, and because they are eminently "classic" . . .

If certain bright people were dreaming of a new classicism, they certainly did not expect a Russian, let alone the author of the SACRE, to bring reality up to their hopes; and it was not beneath the features of OEDIPUS REX that they expected what was called "neo-classicism" to appear. Nevertheless if we reconsider Stravinsky's technical procedures, if we consider the nature of his melodic, harmonic, and rhythmic language from PETROU-SCHKA and RENARD up to NOCES, our surprise will grow less, and I think the Russian origin of this composer will, thus, explain a good deal . . .

"On saisit donc." One seizes then (or shall we translate that: "I think I have given the clue to") the close bond of relationship between Stravinsky's Russian period, and that wherein he turns to the XVIIIth-century masters in his attempt to recreate a style, a common language everywhere understandable, capable of giving the art-work a super-individual structure. Precisely

76

because of his Russianness, he should feel this need of style which torments so many artists today, and he must feel it more profoundly than any one else, because of his systematic and logical spirit . . .

"Classic" usually turns the thought toward order, measure, clarity, equilibrium, serenity. "Romanticism" in these latter days is current rather as pejorative, and is used with a shade of contempt for liberty, exuberance, exaggeration, pathos, sentimentalism, vagueness, unease, lack of limit . . .

I find but one valid distinction between the classic and romantic artist, namely his attitude to reality. The art of the first is a closed world, the art of the second is wide open to life. The art of the first treats reality as mere raw material, which he models according to certain specific formal principles, i. e., principles belonging properly and exclusively to his art, and inoperative and even void of significance outside that art in particular. The classic artist goes *from* the real, to construct a universe in which you will not find one ounce of reality, a universe superposed upon ours; but cut off from it by a wall through which there is no possible passage. What is the real for a musician? Let us say it is the social life as well as the psychological; history as well as his own emotions; the people about him and the products of other arts. If he works on a poetic text or a scenic action, or if he is inspired by an idea, he effects their total transposition by means of certain specific forms which are there at his disposal, thanks to the use of certain conventions which can be used *only* in music, and which deeply modify the very structure of the poetic and scenic elements . . . On this ground one can define classic art as anti-realist, as idealist in the sense that it subjects reality to a group of rules and conventions which destroy the life of the real, i. e., the felt emotion, the meaning of the poetic text, the development of an action, in order to confer upon them a new existence, a new value in a world created by art . . .

The elaboration of musical language, the determining of the pitch, the scales, the melody, etc., are not the product of the single man's choice, but of an artificial creation, coming from what might be called an anti-natural attitude, which has attained its highest development in occidental music . . .

Thus set apart from, or outside the "real" forming a separate sphere under government of an art-made order, the classic work does not come back into life, its action remains purely aesthetic. Here we find the most striking opposition of the classic and romantic types: The romantic tries to act on reality and succeeds. He is "realist" in the very sense that we call the classicist "anti-realist," he welcomes life in his art. Since art is synonymous with artifice, he has to impose certain conventions but he tries to reduce them to a minimum. Hence his ceaseless strife against the rules, his thirst for "liberty" which liberty he has to have in order to give his art "authenticity" or "verity", i. e., bring his work nearer to the diverse, multiform, unstable, fugitive reality. Hence his need to limber up the forms, to break them in order to maintain contact with life which knows none of our measures, categories, or limits. The romantic composer tries to efface the specific character of his particular art which is exactly what the classicist struggles to maintain not only in regard to emotions, sentiments, and ideas which are the source of all artistic production but even in regard to the other arts. The romantic wants to spread out, to abolish the frontiers, to bring in alien elements. He does not think of musicalizing them, for that would mean using the artifices which deform the real, but he dreams of a synthetic art which alone will be able to contain life in all its diversity and richness, by comparison with which the classic work seems to him wholly impoverished . . .

The romantic wants to be more than an artist, he wants his work to acquire a psychological, social, religious, mystical value, hence his conception of art as magic, a magic which should become in his hands an instrument of action . . .

We may consider the art of classic epochs as a distraction, an amusement; for the poet, painter, or musician has no pretension save of creating a stasis or parenthesis in our existence, a pause, an *entr'acte* in which we may rest and breathe.

By this modest attitude one observes that the second world created by the classic artist is only a world of *simulacra*, and differs completely from the world of the romantic who wants to compete with nature or divinity, to avoid *simulacra* or else and at any rate to make them serve some practical purpose. On this count there is a special brand of romantic art: religious art ... By its very drift and tendency religious art, and religious music in particular, aims at transcending aesthetic values, tries to create real states (of mind) and to rejoin life in order to deepen it. In such case one sees a classic spirit like Bach using his art as a means of action but trying to keep as nearly intact as possible the specific forms employable ...

These general remarks ought to lead up to a better understanding of Stravinsky's work and to a more exact estimate of the role it plays in modern music and of its influence on contemporary composers ...

As for the European musical situation when Stravinsky arrived in Paris? It was labelled "romantic" though it showed signs of restlessness against government from Bayreuth, it couldn't get free of the old enchanter's ideas, or more particularly, of his harmonic conceptions. There was a reign of originality, everyone was trying to elaborate his vocabulary, to "find himself," to realize himself in his own way and by an exclusively personal technique ... This aspiration toward liberty, and this revolt against worn-out principles may have been getting ready to adumbrate the birth of a new discipline, but the old shop looked as if it was going to ruin and anarchy prevailed ...

A "discipline" can exist only as a general law, if it is no

more than a group of rules useful or usable only in a particular case it is a misnomer to call it discipline, it is merely a sort of game. The artist no longer sees it as something exterior to himself, alien to his will, to his desires, to all his personality, a thing against which he struggles, to which he must willy-nilly adapt himself, and which precisely on this account, gives his work the anti-natural or above-natural character proper to art. The so-called "free and personal" discipline is merely a systematization or formulation of his aspirations, tastes, mental attitudes. It is the mere illusion of an obstacle, it neither constrains nor limits, but permits him to "realize himself" quite "naturally." This error is so imbedded in us that even today we use it in judging Stravinsky; the man whose work has for years been the utter denial of the romantic principle: "personal discipline freely accepted." How often have we read that "if Stravinsky allows himself new liberties it is only to undertake new obligations"? The writers were obviously trying to defend Stravinsky from charges of anarchy, but the excusings show to what point we are haunted by the individualist-romanticist idea . . .

This romantic individualist spirit shows in the technique? And how?

The romantic is carried toward atonality because the sonorous universe denuded of all tonal organization seems to him much more plastic and supple, and consequently more likely to be mouldable by an artist who is trying to get life into his music and to express by it the immense diversity of the real.

But PETROUSCHKA's revolution backward passed un-understood, it needed the tempests of the SACRE to make people notice that a change had occurred in music . . .

In the SACRE, as we noticed, the harmony and the rhythm attain autonomy, a value of their very own, which one does not find in any later work of Stravinsky and if it is possible to comprehend the orientation of his work as a whole, to graph a main curve of his evolution in which every stage is an entity complete or at least achieved in itself, sufficing to itself, it is precisely by understanding the relations between his melodic, harmonic, rhythmic, and instrumentational elements, and in these the melodic thought gradually establishes exclusive domination. In other words his classic spirit is affirmed long before he turns to the XVIIIth-century masters. It is *because* RENARD, NOCES, and PETROUSCHKA are classic works that their author, at a given moment, felt the absolute necessity of a style and brought to life the ancient traditions . . .

And it is not only the role of the melodic thought which becomes preponderant in Stravinsky, it is the very character of the melody that changes, becoming more finished and consequently more conventional and artificial . . .

Someone will ask why the classic attitude should be tied up with melodic structure, and why the romantic tends to extricate harmony, timbre, and rhythm, from the domination of MELOS? I think there are two reasons for this.

82

Melody is the form of organizing sonority which is furthest removed from reality, the most artificial, and precisely the form by which the sonorous world acquires a specific character. Whatever be the historic origins of song, even if one admit that it began as the howl, i. e., direct, as you might say, physiological expression of emotion; its development is indisputably due to detaching it from its physiological sources and to organizing it according to acoustic and aesthetic principles. Melody is the creation of human intelligence standing up against nature. Nature offers no model but merely imposes certain anatomical and physical conditions which the human mind obeys precisely in order to escape from them and to construct an artificial universe wherein to reign. There is an intellectual part in every melody, and for that reason it demands comprehension from the auditor. It strikes the auditor as melody, succession, only in so far as the auditor is an active collaborator performing a synthesis (as rudimentary as you like) . . .

(I am not talking about technical comprehension; which is a matter for the specialist and which does *not* necessarily go hand in hand with musical comprehension.) As for the great public's taste for melody, it is a matter of only a certain kind of melody to which it has been trained and habituated, and which it likes to *recognize;* once you depart from that type we are all more or less dis-oriented, for the most difficult thing of all to seize is a melody that follows an unexpected course. Thus the first judgment people deliver on a work that they have not understood is that it lacks melody; they said this of Mozart, and they say it today of Ravel, Debussy, and Stravinsky.

If the SACRE finally imposed itself, this was *in spite of* melodic structure and thanks to the hallucinating power of its rhythm, to its glittering timbres, and to its cyclopean chords. But even today the polyphonic idiom of the SACRE remains, in all probability, a closed book to many of its auditors . . . It needed Stravinsky's genius, his radicalism intolerant of compromise, his love of risk, and this absence of aesthetic aristocratism which we have observed in most Russian artists, to bring in the renaissance of a classic art and to reconstitute a style in the midst of this "war of everyone against everyone else" which modern musical life had become . . .

It may seem strange at first sight that a musician of classic type, so caring to emphasize the specific character of his art, a man whose creative thought seems to move exclusively in the realm of sonority, in short a "pure" musician should have felt so constantly drawn to the stage and should have written so many works in which the music finds itself in such close relation with extra-musical elements; plastic forms, scenic action, literary subjects, etc. . . . .

I think there are two reasons for the important role given to the spectacle, the dance, the scenic action in Stravinsky's work. The first is an exterior reason, but external circumstances have always had a great deal to do with Stravinsky's works, many of which were done to order or done with view to a given group of instruments, and the character of the work thus determined in advance, as the APOLLO-MUSAGETES, by the necessity of conforming to certain conditions . . . This never prevents a composer's doing what he wants to do, it even seems that like many other classic artists, Mozart for example, Stravinsky often had to have the limits of his job mapped out before he could get to work; he couldn't be wholly free save in bondage. One may well believe that his close relation with the Diaghileff ballet has greatly favoured the development of Stravinskian art even though it obliged the composer to work for the theatre. I think however that there was an interior reason, possibly several of them, for this theatric production . . .

The composer is, I think, perfectly well aware of how the music of the SACRE was born in him but the genesis of a work, its structure, and its intimate nature are very different things. For example, a work whose first source and origin was an image or a poetic or even abstract idea might perfectly well be an "objective construction" and a piece of autonomous music complete in itself. It all depends on the attitude of the composer, the point of departure need not affect this. Putting aside the SACRE we may admit without endangering his "classicism" that Stravinsky now and again needs a plastic image or a "subject" in order to make the impressions, as he says,

85

"crystallize" and become wholly musical work; that is to say the image, subject, stimulus lets loose the work of musical thought which thereafter affects only the *"matiere sonore,"* the sound-substance (i. e., non-musical cause having effects in exclusively musical sphere).

Stravinsky has carried the concert to the theatre. If Berlioz has theatricized music, Stravinsky has musicalized the theatre, has annexed the stage to music and extended the rule of music over alien domain.

We have already indicated his means for safeguarding the independence of music when faced with texts and scenic action; his scores stand on their own feet when taken away from the stagings for which they were written, and this is because their structure is governed by specific principles and is not merely a function of the stage spectacle. And yet they are theatrical work, conceived to be represented, and there ought to be close relation between the music and the action . . .

The score of the SACRE, or of PETROUSCHKA, NOCES, or MAVRA can perfectly well dispense with the stage set, for everything that Stravinsky has put into them has been completely re-thought and transposed to the plane of sonority and has acquired a musical existence sufficient unto itself. The theatre adds nothing save comment, something to make the music tangible, visible, and rationally explicable.

The putting on the stage of a given work by Stravinsky is in a way re-doing the music from the other end on, reconstituting the world which Stravinsky had dis-composed in order to create a sonorous universe. And this realization in no way jars with the author's intentions. When he writes a score he wants it to be seen, he wants the images and ideas which have served him as pretexts, to take form on the stage, for this autocrat in his own country wants to extend its borders, to bring the concert into the theatre, to musicalize the stage. And he succeeds. The spectacle that takes place in front of us is essentially musical, the world which these theatre people extract from his music bears the indelible imprint of the sonorous "existence" which Stravinsky has given it.

Our composer hardly ever writes dances. NOCES is a cantata. The SACRE is a sort of symphony in two parts, I would call it a symphonic poem if that label hadn't been pre-empted by Liszt and Richard Strauss for a frankly literary and even descriptive type of composition. But the musical dynamism of these two scores of Stravinsky's requires in a way the plastic images, and becomes naturally concrete in postures and dances . . .

His Russian "Oecumenism" and more especially his classic spirit have carried him along in this course, begun with PETROUSCHKA, and never abandoned since, taking him always further along the route of the "commonplace" and toward an ideal universality, realized not by means of an abstraction which would be contrary to the very nature of his art which is by essence concrete, but by recourse to style, attaining type.

If we consider the characters animated by Stravinsky we note the same tendency which has drawn him to modeling his thought on typical forms; all his heroes, however individual, belong to classified types, types in that sense conventional. If as in MAVRA they have a name, the name is a mere label, as Harpagon is a label for the miser. PETROUSCHKA, the Moor, the ballerina are the dolls of Russian puppet-show, in its turn derived from the Italian; the sentimental un-understood lover, his rival the stupid but lucky ladykiller, the inconstant capricious female. In PULCINELLA we find the characters of the Commedia dell'Arte; in RENARD, those of the Russian tales. The devil and the soldier in L'HISTOIRE DU SOLDAT are likewise popular creations. In the SACRE and NOCES there is nothing but gregarious humanity, a collective being, the people whence scarcely emerge the chosen Virgin, the Fiance, the Bride, stripped of all individuality. The actors in MAVRA are the conventional roles of opera bouffe; in OEDIPUS he gives the scene and hero of ancient myth.

There would seem to be nothing more to say about Stravinsky's extraordinary faculty for renewing himself; about the veritable heroism with which he refuses to exploit his successes, but invariably starts fresh and stakes everything boldly as if he were just debutant. For if after long inspection we have managed to find a unity in his work as a whole, every single one of his works has disconcerted us on appearance. The principles of his art which we now think we have discovered have been realized in unexpected fashions, finding their application in new domains and acquiring thereby a development impossible for us to foresee. After every one of these catastrophes in our musical life caused by a new work of Stravinsky's one has gathered one's wits and managed to make out that the author was logical with himself, that he had done what he ought to, all of which didn't in the least prevent one's guessing wrong next time.

But the novelty of APOLLO was a record. And the upsetting of its audience in 1928 was not due to a mere — quite natural — lack of public adaptability. This work really is a "new fact" in the evolution of Stravinskian art . . .

Something much more significant differentiates APOLLO and gives it a value and place apart in Stravinsky's work, revealing perhaps the ultimate secret of man and artist.

From strictly musical angle one sees the relations between APOLLO and the preceding compositions, and one can almost understand how it grew out of the OEDIPUS, as the author applied his principles to a determined domain and adapted his stylistic procedures to a given aim. But nothing in all Stravinsky's other work could have led one to foresee the peace and tenderness of the APOLLO.

Start with FIRE BIRD, PETROUSCHKA, and the SACRE and end with APOLLO! Upset the whole of music, let loose tempests of rhythm, appeal to all the dynamics hidden in sound; exalt

89

force and implacable movement and finally arrive at a modest string orchestra and a work where all is harmony, sweetness, serenity, a form purely lovely and candid, in the etymological sense of that word! What crisis has the composer passed through, that should so completely transform the spirit of his art. Or must we believe that Stravinsky's true face hitherto unknown, and which the artist has been unwilling to show, is that which we find in APOLLO? . . .

Whatever the conditions surrounding the writing of APOLLO it reveals Stravinsky's thirst for renunciation, his need of purity and serenity. In it he achieves the prodigy of being free, spontaneous, and luminous without any apparent effort. What this peace and clarity have cost him can be witnessed only by the long series of precedent works whose exasperated dynamism would almost seem, by comparison with the APOLLO, to be a vain agitation.

During the past ten years there has been a lot of talk about "getting rid" of things, and about *pudeur* or modesty, etc. The least of the Conservatoire pupils was preparing "to renounce." This aesthetic was very convenient for the impotent and the indigent; it was the easy ethic of erecting necessity into virtue and sacrificing what one hadn't got, and even what one didn't know about, riches, power, dangerous superabundance of possessions which alone can give value to asceticism. From this point of view APOLLO contains not only the aesthetic lesson which any work of genius offers, but also a moral, I would even say a religious lesson.

90

It is hard to resist poking into the future; what should we expect from Stravinsky now in the strength of his age and full expansion of his genius? What will his next work be? For our joy or pleasure? Logically, after APOLLO, he ought to give us a Mass, but our logic is probably not his.

EDITOR'S NOTE: Approximately a year after Mr. de Schloezer's article first appeared in this country in *The Dial*, Stravinsky's "Symphony of Psalms" was performed by the Boston Symphony Orchestra under Koussevitzky. The date of the performance was December 19, 1930, and the "Symphony of Psalms" was dedicated to the Boston Symphony Orchestra for the orchestra's fiftieth anniversary. At that time, the late Philip Hale commented in part as follows: "There can scarcely be any question as to the Symphonie de Psaumes being one of the sincerest expressions of Stravinsky's genius and one of his most inspired utterances to the present time."

5

H E N R Y   B O Y S

1934   **Organic Continuity**

Stravinsky has a lively sense of tradition, of the organic continuity of past and present. I believe that he had it naturally, but that believing it to be an essential for himself and for the time, he also cultivated it. For the purposes of his own development and that of his time he could not identify himself with "TRADITION" as it was being contemporaneously developed. Neither could he fall into either of the fundamental errors of revolution or the attempt (so long kept up) to make something out of nothing, with both of which he has been associated. He saw that just as an artist can develop only part of his make-up at a time without stylistic disaster, so he can develop traditionally in accordance with only a limited range of tradition, and that from the whole chaos he must select that which is most congenial to his mind, those of the intelligible devices which can most appropriately help to manifest his imagination and forms.

Stravinsky, as he made quite clear by his "AVERTISSEMENT" (The Dominant, December, 1927), never had the illusion that these devices, which he began to use systematically, constituted any kind of classicism. They do, however, indicate his idea of tradition, which was very different from that of most of his immediate predecessors and contemporaries, the bulk of whom could be divided into traditionalists and decadents, or those who weakened as much as they could assimilate and those who over-developed a particular part of the immediate legacy. Of course, composers now treat Stravinsky's achievements in exactly the same way. Roger Sessions, noticing chiefly the equilibrium, has called this process of Stravinsky's a *reprise de contact,* and Boris de Schloezer, noticing chiefly the devices, "art on art," art, that is, from which the human is excluded because of the use of previously "made-up" material — as it were a double decantation. Both critics acknowledge that Stravinsky is creating, both see his work as something quite new, not to be judged by standards other than its own. But Mr. Schloezer seems to fail to take account of the reason why Stravinsky took this kind of material, or to see that with him it is apparently substituted for more direct feelings, which are in his view not an end, but just the matter of his art.

Nobody was more conscious than Stravinsky of the need in twentieth-century music for stability, equilibrium and those fundamental laws which make music good music as distinct from good art in general. He happened to find in certain masters, especially in those of the classical period, both the devices and the equilibrium which he sought. It happened, then, to be a healthy tendency that he went far away for his matter. For more of our contemporaries who are called emotional composers simply go near at hand for their matter, too near, because the matter is charged with such obvious, identifiable feelings that their works become merely a series of dead feelings, merely labels; each one protruding, so that you cannot see the whole for the parts, the inevitable result of setting out to induce emotions and of allowing material to dictate feeling.

Stravinsky does not use the devices pedantically and academically as would a pasticheur, but creatively, transfusing into them new life. The lack of eclecticism — one might have expected eclecticism to be inevitable — is explained by the fact that all the material, however disparate, passes through his own creative medium and from it issues something different.

Also, by his conviction that the first essential is that all the elements of the music shall be interrelated musically, whether the form (complex of interrelations) corresponds to some external (for instance, dramatic) form or not. So far as he succeeds in this, his work can be called classical, for this and nothing else constitutes classicism. The only impurity for him is when the interrelation is not successful. If his music seems not sufficiently dramatic, too sober, restrained, or mechanical, it is thus because he imagines that in employing any of these qualities he will achieve classical work. His music is clear, but neither does the clarity constitute classicism. Only equilibrium can ever justify the word classical, and equilibrium may be the result of the organization of any kind of material.

Stravinsky never had a grudge against emotion as such. But he very strongly protested against the working-up of emotion as an essential principle and as an end in itself. He knew that emotion is a result of art and helps to form the material of art, but that the deliberate pursuit of that result and the too great reliance upon emotion as a constituent tended to take the mind off the object and thus lessen the intensity of the whole.

His supposed indifference to material is again only an indifference to material regarded as an end instead of as a means. The work makes the material, and not the material the work. "Indifference to material" used by the note-spinners as a slogan means that the material makes the work, not the work the material, for the reason that for them the work is material in itself. Stravinsky never allows his matter to direct or modify the form in his mind, but sets out to relate the matter in such a way as to show forth the most clearly that form. The clarity of the form we see on the paper is the best indication of the authenticity of the conception. For, as Blake says, "the more distinct, sharp, and wiry the bounding line, the more perfect the work of art, and the less keen and sharp, the greater is the evidence of weak imitation, plagiarism, and bungling." So far from there being a hiatus between spontaneity and artifice in his latest work, the nature of his artifice makes an artistic problem strong enough to intensify his creative vigour.

If the above indications are true, then Stravinsky's idea of the way to make music comes near to being a mystical attitude, which is indeed the most probable explanation of his exactitude, of his indifference to human emotion, of his limited appeal, of his intensity, of his asceticism, of his austerity. His latest works follow a sequence. They are a series of proportioned wholes, whose subject-matter is a great variety of different experience, always regarded from the same very specialized angle by a very mature intelligence with immense technical power using extremely sure, perhaps even limiting, methods. Hence, both the disconcerting separateness and the stylistic sameness of each work in the series. Stravinsky has said of this period: "There is nothing to discuss, nor to criticize; one does not

6

EUGENE GOOSSENS

1936　Whole-hearted Champion

It was somewhere about the year 1911, being then a
violinist in the Queen's Hall Orchestra, that I first encoun-
tered the music of Stravinsky. Sir Henry Wood (indomitable
champion of the "new" music in those prewar days) piloted
us through the dangerous reefs of the early SCHERZO FANTAS-
TIQUE, FIREWORKS and FIREBIRD Suite, with that calm, expert

99

hand and unfailing respect for the printed page which still command the admiration of all musicians. Two years later, in the front row of the "stalls" of Drury Lane Theater, I sat open-mouthed with wonderment and heard the twin revelations of PETROUSCHKA and the SACRE DU PRINTEMPS played under the forceful baton of Pierre Monteux, and danced by the Diaghilev Ballets Russes. Five years passed, during which I forsook the violin for opera conducting, and again Diaghilev returned to London, bringing with him the redoubtable Ernest Ansermet to conduct the new PULCINELLA, ROSSIGNOL and repeat performances of Stravinsky's earlier works. I also recall at that time the first (and finest) performance ever given of L'HISTOIRE DU SOLDAT in London under Ansermet, a feat of virtuoso conducting rarely equalled anywhere in my experience.

But this chapter could hardly have come to be written were my experience limited solely to aural — and, consequently, second-hand — contacts with music which in itself requires actual "handling" to appraise the true quality of the stuff of which it is fashioned. I sampled it thuswise when, at Queen's Hall in 1921, the first concert-performance in London of LE SACRE took place under my direction. Again, too, when, from 1922 onwards I conducted the Stravinsky ballets during Diaghilev's London seasons, culminating in the English premiere of LES NOCES at His Majesty's Theater in 1926 (an occasion notable for H. G. Wells' spirited defense of this ballet in the face of an almost completely hostile reception by the critics).

I sample it anew, just as doubtless do many of my colleagues under similar circumstances, each and every time that a work of Stravinsky appears on my programs. For who among conductors of today will deny the stimulus of repeated performances of FIREWORKS, FIREBIRD, PETROUSCHKA, LE SACRE DU PRINTEMPS (somewhat exhausting, this!) PULCINELLA, ROSSIGNOL, APOLLO MUSAGETES and the later works? Which of us has not, at some time or another, sensed the thrilling reaction of this music on our audiences, and chuckled secretly over the breakdown of many an antagonistic and prejudiced point-of-view in face of a convincing performance.

But the responsibility resting on the shoulders of the conductor during the performance of Stravinsky's music is a heavy one. On the one hand, he must avoid the devil of inaccuracy, and on the other, the deep sea of so-called "interpretation." His sense of musical values must be unerring, and his technical equipment vast! Above all, he must be a whole-hearted champion of this music; no mental reservations are possible concerning it. How often have I heard Stravinsky say, in effect, "Either you feel my music, or you don't! Either its logic impresses itself on you, or it doesn't. Either you are musically and technically equipped to conduct it, or you aren't!"

His insistence on the observance of the printed indications in his scores amounts almost to a mania. One day in Paris we were together in his little studio over the Salle Pleyel, a week before he was to play his PIANO CONCERTO at a concert of mine at Queen's Hall, in 1929. I had never conducted the work, and therefore availed myself of our few minutes together to ask him one or two questions concerning "tempi," phrasing, etc. Remarking that I was puzzled by the dynamics of a certain sequence in the finale, and after much discussion and much re-playing of the passage in question (Stravinsky, incidentally, is a formidable pianist) he suddenly jumped from his seat, good-humouredly thumped the keyboard, and with an expression of tolerant exasperation exclaimed, "But, my dear fellow, play just what's written, and stop *worrying!!*" I took his advice, with the best possible results . . .

Granted that works such as LE SACRE, NOCES and the aforementioned CONCERTO present more surface problems of a rhythmical nature to the conductor than almost any music hitherto written, I think it will be found that these problems will be quickly disposed of from the moment it is realized that, unless otherwise indicated, no deviation in tempo from the unit of rhythm can ever be tolerated. No conductor can hope to approximate Stravinsky's intentions who, while beating a succession of measures of, let us say, the following time-values: 3/16, 4/16, 2/16, 5/16, 3/16, 5/16, 7/16 — is incapable of preserving the rhythmic integrity of the semi-quaver throughout. Likewise, there can be no place in this music for "interpretational" effects or any play of sentiment on the part of the conductor. Small wonder that, in the first volume of his autobiography, the composer expresses himself uncompromisingly on the subject of individual "readings." "It is enough to cite Beethoven, and to take as an illustration his 8TH SYMPHONY, which bears the composer's own metronomic directions. But are they heard? There are as many different renderings as there are conductors." Or still later, "Have you heard *my* FIFTH? *my* EIGHTH? That is a phrase that has become quite usual in the mouths of these gentlemen, and their mentality could not be better exemplified." No mincing words here!

On the other hand, the idea is current in many quarters that subtleties of expression have no place in Stravinsky's music. Anyone who has conducted this music will immediately be able to refute such a ridiculous notion. It seems to have arisen from a misconception of the extreme economy of statement to be found in the later works from the composer's pen. There is as much scope for real expression in a performance of APOLLO, OEDIPUS REX, the SYMPHONIE DES PSAUMES and PERSE-PHONE, as in the BERCEUSE from the FIREBIRD, but there is absolutely no room for *sentimentality*: a commodity as foreign to the work of Stravinsky as it is essential to a drawing-room ballad. I must leave to other pens the task of estimating these formidable works at their true musical value, but writing as a conductor with some understanding of the composer's aims and intentions, I emphatically protest against the later work of Stravinsky being dubbed the dessicated, tenuous, devitalized thing it is represented to be by so many of the knowing ones!

103

True, many find the later works unsympathetic (it takes all kinds to make a world!) but no musician can deny the mastery with which the composer has set down, clearly, precisely and uncompromisingly that which is as logical and outspoken in content as anything I know of in music.

Obviously it is music which will tolerate no virtuoso tricks from the conductor. Approach it with a lack of conviction, or try to superimpose upon it the old conductorial formulae — with one eye to the effect on the public — and this music will fail utterly in its message. In so doing, it will also administer to its would-be "interpreter" a venomous psychological backlash which will not easily be forgotten.

In other words, Stravinsky has cooked the dinner; it is for the conductor to see that it be served to the consumer precisely as it left the hands of the chef, with no re-heating and, above all, no additional "sauce piquante."

7

A R T H U R   B E R G E R

1943   The Stravinsky Panorama

Igor Stravinsky presents the curious paradox of a composer who, after being attacked on the grounds that he was too far in advance of his time, is now unjustly criticized for being too far behind it. And, odd as it may seem, the origin of both onslaughts is the same: the initial reluctance of the appreciators of any art to readjust themselves to the altering values which the constant probing of the artist must inevitably engender. For the artist by nature is one who sees ever new ways of re-combining existing material, that is, because he is searching for the *perfect* way of forming this material.

105

Thus, the long line of masterpieces Stravinsky has achieved since he left behind him the currently more accepted idiom of the ballets for Diaghilev which he wrote just before World War I, is often said merely to echo the great music of older composers as a compensation for an attrition of his own creative faculty. But this merely indicates that listeners have not yet adjusted their eyes to this remarkable new light (so to speak) in order to get the particular curve of uniqueness which each new work embodies, just as thirty years ago, they were similarly dazzled by a different kind of new light to such an extent that they could not make out the proper contours of the elements which comprise THE RITE OF SPRING and heard only disjointed cacophony where they now hear rich and profoundly stirring harmony and rhythm. (There are, of course, those who do not get beyond THE FIREBIRD and who cling to the ridiculous notion that Stravinsky's decline started after this work. But the numbers of these have diminished rapidly, especially since Disney's spade work in disseminating THE RITE OF SPRING in his "Fantasia.") One can already see THE SYMPHONY OF PSALMS (1930) undergoing this orientation.

The chief cause of this myopia is prejudice. Past experience leads us to expect certain things to recur, and a normal human lassitude rebels against the exertion of an effort required to orient ourselves to new things. Even more prejudiced than the average listener, are the teachers and critics to whom this listener looks for guidance. These benighted individuals have

106

arrived at a crystallized notion of what good music is, a kind of rule of thumb system adapted to quick application to make their job easier. New types of music may upset their system if it is not sufficiently plastic to cope with the range of situations. This means extra work for them. They are, therefore, so suspicious when anything new comes along, that they approach it with a prejudice and conviction in advance that good music cannot be composed according to the new standards proposed. Their distrust of the new method and the new intentions themselves often blocks them from listening to what has been accomplished *within* the new method. What they condemn as bad is often something which they have not even given a fair trial.

This article aims at nothing more arduously than at dispelling the invidious myth that Stravinsky's latest period is an unnatural and unfertile development. On the contrary, what seems so very evident in his development is the organic advancement from one type of music to another, determined by the nature of his background, the progress of history, and the quest for the most permanent musical principles. This is no less true of his transition from LES NOCES to the OCTET than of his transition from FIREBIRD to PETROUCHKA. The whimsical about-face, which is so often insisted upon by critics, is in reality not there. Let us, then, observe the sequence of what is commonly referred to as Stravinsky's various styles, noticing especially that this inevitable continuity exists.

The segregation of a composer's works into separate groups

as products of different periods is often forced and arbitrary. Even in the normal evolution of every artist, there are no clear boundaries between the three inevitable stages: the student days of assimilation; the achievement of a personal idiom; the final reaching towards the highest values after so much has been eliminated by experience. Qualities of one stage flow over generously into another. In Stravinsky's case, what may be at bottom no more than this normal curve from student days to profound seriousness, seems, however, to subject itself more to the insertion of boundary lines; and it is important to have these clearly in mind to avoid confusion. Different people often seem to be talking about different men when they discuss Stravinsky, according to whether their knowledge and interest extends to THE FIREBIRD, THE RITE OF SPRING, or THE SYMPHONY OF PSALMS, which clearly represent three consecutive periods according to the largest view of his career. (A fourth period can easily be dismissed as a formative one, namely, the early period of a Symphony in the nineteenth century manner. The departure from the normal curve of three divisions seems less odd when it is recognized that THE FIREBIRD was part of a relatively brief stage.)

For a Russian composer, a thorough master of his craft at twenty-eight, and a student of the recently deceased Rimsky-Korsakov, to have written THE FIREBIRD in 1909-10 in a post-Rimsky and somewhat "impressionist" idiom, was a most inevitable phenomenon. As at all epochs of musical history, a great artist has singled out the most vital and fertile tendency of his time, and through it, developed his own personality. But even among the scintillating Rimskyan orchestral sounds, the individual hand of Stravinsky was already evident: a more terse statement of thematic material and a frenetic quality that looks forward to THE RITE OF SPRING. THE FIREBIRD was the culmination of a style that was being perfected for some three years during which the chief accomplishments were the SCHERZO FANTASTIQUE, the fairly well known FIREWORKS, the delightful PASTORALE with a somewhat Rimskyan orientalism in relief against the crisp woodwind writing of the later OCTET, and the first act of ROSSIGNOL which, as completed after PETROUCHKA in the form of symphonic poem, obviously serves as a link with the subsequent period, especially in the daring of some of its effects and the sober control of the beautiful subdued trumpet theme near the end.

As we proceed from this period to the one which ranges from PETROUCHKA, through the charming opera of 1922, MAVRA, we may find ourselves having a sensation of leaving a sumptuous interior for a healthy and athletic outdoor atmosphere. Stravinsky had not entirely deserted the typically Russian preoccupation with color and instrumentation, by any means. The traditional folk element of Rimsky-Korsakov and, still more notably, of Moussorgsky, was intensified. Whereas Rimsky-Korsakov had used folk tunes with conservatory refinement, Stravinsky captured, especially in RENARD and LES NOCES, the whole buoyant and convivial atmosphere, even to the point of an artistically handled and tasteful garrulousness. There is clearly reflected in this period the childhood experience of the Russian countryside such as the composer describes at the outset of his lucid and informative autobiography: for example, the weird music of the peasant who pressed the palms of his hands under his arm-pits and brought forth "from under his shirt a series of rather suspect sounds but very rhythmic and which one may euphemistically quality as 'nurse's kisses.' It amused me very much and, at home, I applied myself very zealously to imitating this music, so much and so well that I was forbidden to use an accompaniment so indecent." I have been told by Nadia Boulanger (the celebrated French teacher of so many American composers, who, moreover, knows Stravinsky's music and intentions better than anyone, perhaps, but the composer himself), that he was also profoundly impressed by the peasant accordions, in which one chord is heard wheezing out while the other wheezes in. There is an intermediate moment when both sounds clash. What many have regarded as an obstinate and hyper-theoretical superimposing of one chord on another to get a rather dissonant effect, would seem then to be a means of achieving the more exact curve of a common and very human experience. It is this device that gives the well known Danse Russe for the dancing bears in PETROUCHKA its odd sound. And even in the latest period we still find evidences of its use — which is just one of many indications that this music is not as divorced from human experience as some insist.

A new element in this period of THE RITE OF SPRING is a far greater control. The Neo-Catholic French philosopher, Jacques Maritain, who first condemned this work for a Wagnerian materialism and sensuous hysteria, later admitted an underlying order and nobility which would preclude the possibility of even the most ardent religious being shocked by what was for a long time regarded as orgiastic and almost obscene music. Carl van Vechten has given a vivid account of its premiere, at which the man sitting behind him beat out the barbaric rhythms on van Vechten's head in a frenzy typical of a widespread response and resembling the jive sessions of James or Goodman at the Paramount. Stravinsky left the hall in disgust at the "very first measures of the prelude which immediately stirred up laughter and mockery," according to his own description of the event. "These manifestations, at first, isolated, soon became general and, provoking on the other side counter-demonstrations, transformed themselves quickly into a frightful pandemonium." The dancers were frantic, being able to hear neither the music nor Nijinsky in the wings counting for them, with the composer at his side holding his coat-tails to prevent him from leaping onto the stage to make a scene.

Those who accuse Stravinsky of being an erstwhile "revolutionary" who has now made a somersault to outright "conservatism" as a deliberate and sensational gesture forget that at the time of the premiere he welcomed the action of his friend, Ravel, who, as Stravinsky pointed out in his recently published

Harvard lectures (Harvard University Press), intervened "almost alone in the tumult of these contradictory opinions" to set things right. The French composer pointed out that the novelty resided "not in the writing, in the instrumentation, in the technical apparatus of the work, but in the musical entity."

The innovations of this period were normal extensions of practices handed down. Stravinsky, for example, combined into a single tonal mass, chords which other composers had sounded successively. The principle of relation, in a sense, did not change. His reaction against the saccharine of late romanticism, moreover, was a continuation of what Satie had already begun. But in place of Satie's cynical nihilism, there was a more positive substitution of athleticism or mordant harmonies for the over-caressing sonorities of the 1900's. This much he did share with Satie, and with Picasso, however: he reinstated black, white and the primary colors which eighteenth century musicians had used to such advantage, and which should never have been abandoned in the first place for a constant blending. He went further than Satie in his use of the contrasts that could be obtained from their juxtaposing, after the eighteenth century manner.

Whether consciously or not, then, he was approaching the classical composers with whom he was to ally himself openly from 1923, during his latest period. In restricting himself, at times, to a kind of harmonic movement akin to running in place, he was closer to Mozart than to Wagner who was always chasing after a constantly receding harmonic goal. (This is what may be technically characterized as staying close to a tone center, as opposed to Wagner's constantly wandering center.) In another sense, the pre-1923 Stravinsky was close to the post-romantics in their pre-occupation with color, and the final break with romanticism after 1923 resided mainly in the substitution of something parallel to classical development where this pre-occupation had formerly appeared. At the same time "local" national color, which was a romantic contrivance, gave way to an international style.

Critics claim that this resumption of classical principles involves an unnatural retrogression to an era with which we have no vital connection. But the principles are related to a permanent aspect of good music and are determined by the nature of tones. They are not peculiar to the eighteenth century, but merely happened to be most thoroughly understood in that century. There is a certain amount of deliberate reflection of eighteenth century clichés in Stravinsky's later works, but they are quite distinct from the underlying principles — though the interest in the former is not unrelated to that in the latter. And those who accept his compiling of Russian and French traditional tunes in PETROUCHKA, or his use of folklike themes in THE RITES OF SPRING, cannot legitimately object to his embracing a Bachian turn in the VIOLIN CONCERTO or a *concerto grosso* style in DUMBARTON OAKS or the DANSES CONCERTANTES. What matters most is not who has created the fragmentary melodic elements,

113

but the whole complex in which they are involved. A Beethoven Symphony is more than the sum of its parts.

This can be clearly illustrated in a satirical work like THE CARD GAME (which it should be emphasized, however, is satirical in the same way that great literary works like Gulliver's Travels or Tristram Shandy are, while at the same time being profound). Thus, the slight suggestion of the so-called Victory motif in the last movement is heightened by the irony of relations and frank similarities pointed up between it, a cheap march, a popular Rossini theme, a later magnificent Stravinskyian development.

Essentially, PETROUCHKA has more in common with PULCINELLA (1920) than with the recent SYMPHONY IN C (1940), although of the two earlier works, the one is based largely on Russian folk tunes and the other on themes of Pergolesi. The compilation of themes of a classical composer does not make PULCINELLA classical in the same way that the symphony is. One might just as well say that Stravinsky became a "neo-romantic" in 1928 when he used Tschaikowsky's themes for LE BAISER DE LA FÉE. In all these works, it is not simply what he *used,* but *what* he *did* that obviously makes them what they are. And if it is true, as it is often insisted, that Stravinsky went to folk music and other composers to compensate for the dearth of a natural melodic gift, it is also true that he has finally come around by sheer exertion of will to writing his own magnificent long lines of the utmost inevitability (e.g., listen to the whole Pas d'action from APOLLON).

Portrait of Stravinsky
by Edward Weston in 1936

Stravinsky talks with students at the University of Illinois, where for the first time Stravinsky conducted an orchestra of advanced student players. Photograph by John Vachon

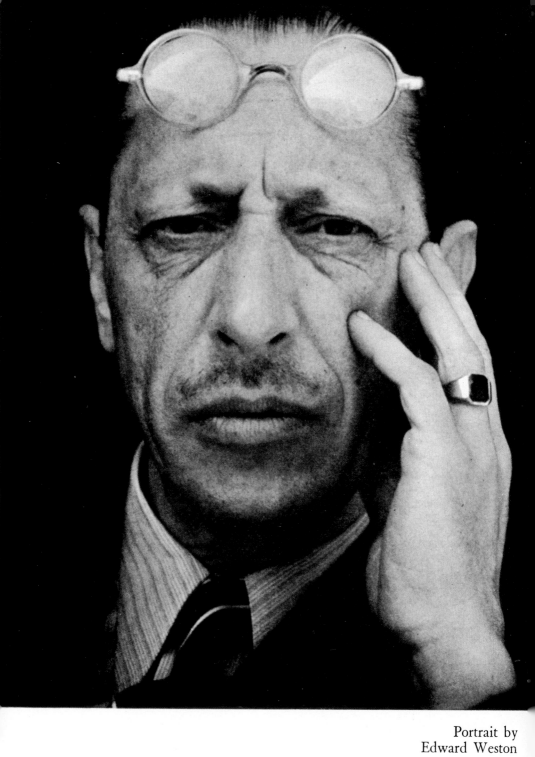

Portrait by
Edward Weston

Portrait by
Arnold Newman in 1949

Stravinsky as the orchestra sees him. (John Vachon)

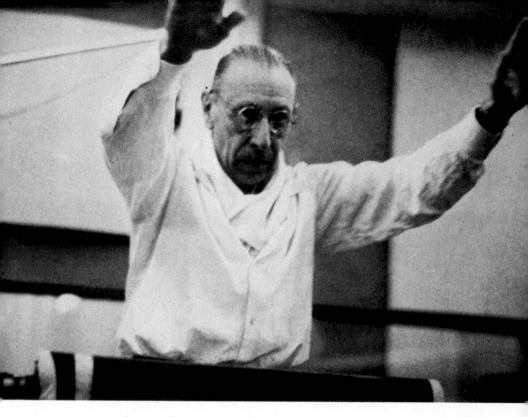

Stravinsky conducts a recording rehearsal. Photograph by Fred Plaut

Stravinsky at his home in Los Angeles

Dynamics at rehearsal. (John Vachon)

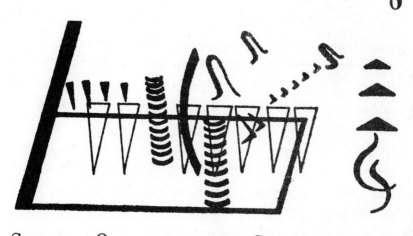

8

SIR OSBERT SITWELL

1947   **English Discernment**

"I have a burning admiration for Stravinsky, and would not like not to be included in any tribute to the greatest living musical genius."

So write Sir Osbert Sitwell to Merle Armitage during the preparation of this book. For permission to quote from Sir Osbert's book, "Great Morning!", the editors wish to express their appreciation for the following excerpts not only to the author but to Little, Brown & Company, and to the Atlantic Monthly Press. (Copyright 1947 by Sir Osbert Sitwell.)

"And so, on this occasion, too, when I had booked a solitary seat for Covent Garden, I had expected, I suppose, something of the same kind: [a production of MADAME BUTTERFLY] for I was aware that as a rule, ballet was interpolated in operas, and I knew nothing of the program . . . Detained at Aldershot, I did not reach the theater until the moment when the curtain was going up, for the first time in London, on L'OISEAU DE FEU. I had been so tired by the day's riding that I had nearly decided not to go — but directly the overture began to be played, I came to life. Never until that evening had I heard Stravinsky's name; but as the ballet developed, it was impossible to mistake the genius of the composer, or of the artist who had designed the setting; a genius plainly shared, too, by the chief dancers and the choreographer. Genius ran through the whole of this ballet. Nevertheless Stravinsky towered above the others, a master. It may be that today the music of this particular piece sounds almost traditional when compared with his later work, such as LE SACRE DU PRINTEMPS or LES NOCES, but as I heard it and watched the accompanying dances, I was aware that for the first time I had been given the opportunity of seeing presented upon the stage a work of art, imbued with originality and with the spirit of its own day; not a tawdry glut of color and rushing movement — like Reinhardt's spectacles, that had somehow burst right out of the theater into enormous barns like Olympia; with them I was already acquainted — but a performance in which every gesture, every line, every tone, meant something; a work of art that could not have existed before, and would cease to be given in its perfection, within the brief season of the dancers' finest span. Those working in the fields of art possess the same saturation with it that sets the Greeks apart as a race; and with Russians, as with Greeks, the theater is the real dynamic center of their arts . . . The long, plangent ripple of the harp strings as the Firebird entered appeared to offer to one some hidden meaning, just as the gathering of ogres and sinister satellites round the crouching, wasplike figure of their baleful master, Koscheii (played that night by the great Cecchetti), seemed to bear some relation to life as I knew it . . . The gates of life could be opened, if one possessed the key (what could I do?), and the powers of evil, chaotic and uncreated, ill-proportioned and anomalous, could be put to flight by one feather plucked from that rare bird. The raging of the old tyrant, and his sycophantic cronies and dependents, *could* be faced. Now I knew where I stood. It would be, for so long as I lived, on the side of the arts. (They needed champions, as well as exponents; at least my life in Barracks had taught me that.) I would support the artist in every controversy, on every occasion.

* * * * *

"In the same theater in which Chaliapin appeared, on other nights or at other hours, another art, besides opera, was to be seen in its perfection: the ballet that blooms for a year, it seems, every century, was enjoying one of its culminations. It becomes inevitable, when writing of it at this time, that the word *genius* should recur with frequency, almost with monotony, in these few pages, for no other word can describe the quality of the chief dancers or the influences at work: Stravinsky, Diaghilev, Karsavina, Fokine, and Nijinsky . . . Of all the productions of these years, PETROUCHKA must be mentioned at the head of the list; the music the first work of a composer of genius grown to his full stature. (L'OISEAU DE FEU, wonderful though its music is, was the more derivative work of a very young man); as moving and symbolic a creation of its time as Mozart's DON GIOVANNI. I have seen other great dancers, but never one inspired as was Nijinsky; I have seen other great dancers play PETROUCHKA, but never one who, with his rendering of a figure stuffed with straw, struggling from the thraldom of the puppet world towards human freedom, but always with the terrible leaden frustration of the dummy latent in his limbs, the movement of them containing the suggestion of the thawing of ice at winter's edge, evoked a comparable feeling of pathos. This ballet was, in its scope as a work of art, universal; it presented the European contemporary generation with a prophetic and dramatized version of the fate reserved for it, in the same way that the legend of the Minotaur had once summed up, though after the event and not before it, the fate of several generations of Greek

118

youths and maidens. The music, traditional yet original, full of fire and genius, complication and essential simplicity, held up a mirror in which man could see, not only himself, but the angel and ape equally prisoned within his skin. The part of Petrouchka showed Nijinsky to be a master of mime, gesture, drama, just as, in pure dancing, his rendering of the Spirit of the Rose, in LE SPECTRE DE LA ROSE, was the climax of romantic ballet.

* * * * *

"Three nights after the introduction of LE COQ D'OR, we were given another combined opera and ballet; Stravinsky's LE ROSSIGNOL: a work now rather seldom mentioned, and perhaps in its first version not altogether successful. It did not manifest the miraculous sense of growth, of fullness of the earth, that LE SACRE DE PRINTEMPS possessed, of the blocks of ice bumping and clanging together in the freed rivers, of the furry buds bursting from their boughs with the loud grunts and cacophonies of spring: it had not PETROUCHKA's drama and pathos, nor the mellifluous enchantment of L'OISEAU DE FEU, yet it had about it a kind of pure, flat, two-dimensional beauty, very rare and full of delicacy . . . At the end of the performance I was excited to see the great Russian composer, the master of the epoch, walk before the curtain. Slight of frame, pale, about thirty years of age, with an air both worldly and abstracted, and a little angry, he bowed back with solemnity to the clustered, nodding tiaras and the white kid gloves, that applauded him sufficiently to be polite: yet for all their genteel tepidity, how little did the audience comprehend the nature of the great musician to whom they were doing honor, or the often eschatological import of his work.

By one of the most singular paradoxes in the history of art, the tiaras and the gloves at least were *there,* doing him honor from the stalls and boxes; whereas the audience that should have been in their place, the advanced painters and musicians of England, convinced that nothing esthetically good could come from such a quarter, rigorously abstained from being present at any performance at Drury Lane and Covent Garden. Thus the enthusiasts for beauty missed, for some years, the most vital influence in the art world."

9

A A R O N C O P L A N D

1949 The Personality of Stravinsky

For almost thirty years I have wondered about the exact nature of the personality of Stravinsky. Everyone agrees that Stravinsky possesses one of the most individual natures of our time. But to get at the essence of it is another matter.

Certain great composers are literally drenched in their own personal atmosphere. One thinks immediately of Chopin, or the later Beethoven, or the mature Wagner. On the other hand, if you don't listen closely, there are times when you might mistake Mozart for Haydn, or Bach for Handel, or even Ravel for Debussy. I cannot ever remember being fooled by the music of Stravinsky. It invariably sounds like music that only he could have written.

Why? I'm sure I don't know . . . but I keep wondering about it. Musicians will tell you that you must take the music apart, see how it is made, then put it together again, and you will have the answer. I've tried it, but it doesn't really work. Knowing Stravinsky the man helps a little, but not enough. At home he is a charming host, a man with clearly defined ideas and a sharp tongue . . . but the music seems to exist on a supra-personal plane, in an aural world of its own.

It is his work of the last few years that holds the mystery tightest. One thinks of the ODE, the MASS, the ballet ORPHEUS . . . these works, in some curious way, seem strangely removed from everyday "events" — and yet they remain profoundly human. Sobriety is the keynote — it seems hardly possible to create a music of less sensuous appeal. Nevertheless, there are moments of an enriched texture — all the more rare and precious because they seem measured out so carefully. In these works thought and instinct are inextricably wedded, as they should be.

These few remarks hardly touch the surface of the problem. Perhaps it is just because the secret cannot be extracted that the fascination of Stravinsky's personality continues to hold us.

122

10

N I C O L A S N A B O K O F F

1949 Christmas with Stravinsky

"Dear Nika Dimitrievitch,

"Yes, of course we will be expecting you for Christmas. You will stay right here with us. You will sleep on the sofa on which slept Nadia Boulanger, Olson,

Auden and others. Huxley was too long. I hope it will be long enough for you. (What is your height?)

"You and Balanchine will probably take the Super-Chief, which gets you into Pasadena at 8:13 a.m. We will meet you *there*. (Pasadena is the last station before Los Angeles and closer to us.)

"Please don't disappoint us this time — *come!* Vera sends greetings.

"Yours,

"Igor Str."

[The letter was in Russian, written on one side of a half-sheet of airmail paper, in Stravinsky's jagged handwriting, and in very black ink. The sentence, "What is your height?" was in red pencil on the left hand margin, with an asterisk following the previous sentence and a red-pencil tracer leading to it. The sentence about Pasadena was in blue pencil, upside down in the top right hand corner. A blue asterisk and a blue-pencilled tracer connected it with the previous sentence. The word *zdýes* (here) was underlined with a blue pencil; the word *tam* (meaning *there* and referring to Pasadena) was boxed in a blue-pencilled frame; the word *priýezjäite!* (come!) was heavily underlined in red pencil. The whole little sheet gave the impression of compact and calculated orderliness and with its several colors, looked like a gay and nervous drawing.]

"Dear Igor Fëdorovitch,

"Please forgive this late answer, but I wanted to be definite and only yesterday did I decide to go *définitivement*. Also, Balanchine wants to "rest in a train" (Sic!) whereas I want to fly, so we compromised: we go on the train, we fly back. We couldn't get any reservations on either "Chiefs." Balanchine's Dr. B. got us a drawing room in a "through" car on some kind of a "Limited." I believe it leaves sometime around 4 p.m. from Grand Central, but I don't know when it arrives in Los Angeles. My understanding is that this train doesn't go through Pasadena. We will wire you from Chicago.

"Auden, who is back today, tells me that you need scores of Handel's operas. Do you have *Caesar* and *Rosamunde?* If not, I will bring them. How is the libretto? Much love to Vera Arturovna and yourself.

"Yours,

"N. N."

"Dear Nika Nabokov,

"We are glad you are coming. Don't be late to the train. If you are going via Grand Central it is probably the Commodore Vanderbilt which has a "through" car. It makes connections in Chicago with the Grand Canyon Limited (which is a *slow* train). The Commodore Vanderbilt arrives in Chicago at 8.30 Chicago time (I just verified it on the time table), and the Grand Canyon leaves Chicago at noon. Thus, leaving the 19th at 4.30 p.m. (N.Y. time), you will arrive in Los Angeles (L.A. time) on the 22nd at 11 a.m. We will meet you at the station unless Maria Balanchine meets George in her car. In that case, she could easily drop you at our house, which is on her way anyhow.

"We both liked Auden very much and I believe the libretto will be very good. Yes, of course, bring all you have of Handel's operas. All the rest we will discuss here. Come, come quickly. Greetings from both of us.

"Yours,

"I. S."

"P. S. [on the left-hand margin in black pencil] Ask George to get [now in red and blue pencil] 2 bottles of Eau de Geniévre — it is *better* than vodka. I can't find it here. George will know where to get it. *priŷezjäite!*"

The drawing room of the "through" car disappointed me. In my imagination I had devised a luxury model bristling with chromium, beds sliding down or arising from under modern plush upholstery, and discreet invisible plumbing and air conditioning. Instead, our room was the usual wan green, musty-smelling compartment of a tubercular Pullman car: coughing plumbing, clanking piping and wiggly neurotic fan.

Balanchine, having "organized" the fancy-colored Christmas packages on the racks ("Best Wishes to Vera Arturovna—V. K."; "Merry Xmas, expecting you soon in New York—Vittorio," etc.), installed himself opposite me with a purr-like grunt. Soon his nose nodded to the rhythm of the car and the pages of the *Daily Mirror* wilted in his plant-like hands.

The train slipped out of the tunnel. The rush of haggard shrubbery and disconsolate housing abruptly shifted to the calm flow of the Hudson, its black surface chopped by slushy icefloats.

This was my first trip to California. I had never wanted to go. Up to the last minute I could not make up my mind whether to give in to the persuasion of a convenient neuralgia and send Balanchine off alone. The whole trip appeared silly and extravagant. To surrender oneself to some three night-days of boredom, restlessness and insomnia in "through" cars, "luxury" diners ("Sorry sir, no more roast beef." "Sorry sir, they forgot to put on the wine in Chicago") and "strato-stuffed" airliners; to become subject to the dispensation of discomfort by railroad and airplane companies, only for the pleasure of four or five days in California (unfamiliar surroundings, dubious landscape) seemed capricious indeed. True enough, at the other end of the journey there were the two Stravinskys, whom I liked so much and whom I had come to know so well during the years of their American "retreat." Auden had described to me how warmly they received their friends, how simple and gay Igor Fëdorovitch can be in his tiny home. Then, too, I remembered the stern Stravinskyan warning, "Do not disappoint us this time. *Come!* [or else . . .]," and of course the relentless fascination which he held for me as for most of the musicians of my generation. To see him in his house, to observe him at work in his studio, to talk to him for long hours and follow the trail of his punctual, agile thought, enlivened with succulent metaphor ("Can you imagine what it means for me to conduct in the City Center, with its orchestra pit like a men's room and no acoustics at all? It is like putting a new Rolls Royce on Russian roads." Or about the Berkshire Festival: "It is perfectly all right, but why should contrabasses practice outdoors under pine trees? After all, they are not herbiverous instruments."), and above all, to scrutinize his latest scores — all this seemed enticing enough to outweigh the apparent absurdity of the tedious journey.

Taking a long train trip is like cooking a steak. Up to a point, while the steak is still rare, it preserves its identity with the animal of its origin; as soon as it turns brown it moves closer to the animal who will consume it.

Thus with my journey: Sometime in Chicago, between

128

8.30 a.m., when I peered out of our overheated sleeper and saw coats, hats and briefcases moving in wintry vapors towards the stairway in the LaSalle Street Station, and 12.30, when Balanchine and I, frosted by Lake Michigan winds, returned from a lonely tour through the Art Institute (where delicate French midsummers strip-teased from behind Renoirish nudes and iridescent Seuratic Sunday strollers), my thoughts had veered from New York and our hectic departure, to the unknown Stravinsky home in Hollywood. Soon I began to wonder if they could really put me up, if it were convenient for them. It seemed a dreadful imposition to use their sofa, particularly during Christmas week, when they would surely have many guests. Would it have been wiser to stay at a hotel? I asked Balanchine.

"Oh, no," he said, "they love to have guests. He, in particular. Don't worry, he won't let you alone for a minute; he will talk to you day and night and ask you a million questions. They will drive you around Hollywood and take you to the best restaurants to dinner. In the morning you will have breakfast with him and his parrot and you will see him do his Hungarian calisthenics. You know he is well-built [George clasped his arms] and phenomenally strong, with a wrestler's biceps. He jumps like a ball, walks on his head and does push-ups with the ease of a twenty-year-old. And besides, "he will play you his new scores," he added sententiously, "it will do you good to look at them carefully. Don't think of going to a hotel. You will offend him and he will never forgive you."

129

All along the way my thoughts buzzed around Stravinsky. I thought of his extraordinary destiny, how strange, how brilliant and how perplexing it has been. A true and earthy child of that miscarriage of history — the Russian civilization of the nineteenth century — he reflected both its creative dynamism and its refinements. Stravinsky has been one of the earliest Great Refugees of our ungrateful modern times. He left old-fashioned, miasmic Imperial Russia, which had no real use for him, in the first decade of our century and he never returned to any of the Russias which have since appeared on the Eurasian plain. He has little use for any of them, least of all for the various Red ones, even for his Russian memories, and he is altogether free of any romantic Ulyssean longing. For Stravinsky, Russia is a language, which he uses with superb, gourmand-like dexterity; it is a few books; Glinka and Tchaikowsky.

In the years between 1908 and 1913, Stravinsky became famous in the old-world capital of Paris, where a wave of infatuation with exotics brought about the "discovery" of Russian music, painting, opera and ballet.

These were the true *années des Ballets Russes,* as any Parisian old-timer will tell you. The astonishing success of Diaghilev's opera and ballet venture in Paris, which began in 1906 with the production of BORIS GODUNOV and culminated in 1912 and 1913 with the productions of PETROUSCHKA and THE RITES OF SPRING, turned the West toward the 75-year-old Russian

Art, "the new Eastern enchantment full of rich, flashy colors and tempestuously wild or languorously melancholic music" (quoting an imaginary Parisian music column of the time). This was approximately the time when in America musicians' names began to end in *ov's, itzky's* and *owsky's* instead of in the old familiar *rosch's, ann's, er's, elli's* and *ini's;* the time of the first invasion by Sachas, Grishas, Mishas and Jaschas.

During these years, Stravinsky, a young man of twenty-five from the land of the tzars, boyars, samovars, ballerina mistresses and vodka, attracted notice as the most famous *fauve* of Western music, the leader of its most radical movement.

In 1913 he shocked the congregation of Paris balletomanes by his RITES OF SPRING. The scandal of the first performance of this work at the Theatre des Champs Elysées, the yelling, whistling and the ensuing scuffle (some fifty people got undressed to the bone and landed in the Commissariat de Police on the rue Havre Commartin), has never been surpassed, not even by the historical scandal of the first performance of TANNHÄUSER (that time the Jockey Club offered to its opera-going members elegant silver whistles with the inscription *"pour siffler 'Tannhäuser' "*). From then on Stravinsky's leadership of modern Western music became incontestable. As years went by this position of leadership gained more prestige and received a greater and deeper respect mixed at times with envy, jealousy or limitless adulation. His reputation spread over the world in a similar and perhaps somewhat broader way

131

than the fame of Picasso, his close friend and collaborator. Every new work of Stravinsky's was a major event; his Parisian adepts, the "inner circle" of his admirers, acclaimed him as the greatest composer of the time. His music was eagerly awaited by an enormous public and equally eagerly discussed. There was hardly a music magazine in Europe which did not discuss his art in every issue; scores of books appeared about his music. Each of his new "lines," each attempt at a new style became immediately the topic of fierce discussion and the musical fashion of the year.

No sooner did the chestnuts begin to burgeon along the boulevards of Paris than the international musical intelligentsia would be seething with rumors about the new Stravinsky ballet or concert piece which was to have its first performance each year at the end of May. I remember the unique, the unforgettably pure excitement (so totally devoid of any non-musical considerations), of these first performances of Stravinsky's music, the electric tension of the audience and the ensuing ovations.

A real commotion occurred when, in the early 'twenties, Stravinsky shook off the domination of Russian folk lore, when he stopped using Russian subjects altogether, when he turned toward the Western tradition and started writing music akin in style and spirit to the baroque period, the period of Bach, Handel and Scarlatti. Numerous people were so deeply shocked at this new monster, half-jazz, half-Bach; half-modern man, half-powdered wig, that they developed an intense and a prolonged heart-bleed. They bled at the loss of the "Russian Stravinsky" (the Stravinsky of THE FIREBIRD), they bled at the horror of this perverse new thing which, for want of a better term (or rather, for lack of imagination), was christened "neo-classicism." The bleeding persisted and in some cases developed into hemophilia. Traces of it can still be found, for example, in the pages of the New York *Times*. It manifests itself in an angry, resentful and disillusioned denial of nearly all that Stravinsky has written since he abandoned the sacred soil of Russian subject matter.

Today, many still hate his music for many contradictory reasons. He deceived the congenital lover of Russia (not the new, but the exotic, fairy-tale Russia of wide spaces and *âme slave*), he enraged the extremists by his respect for and his return to tradition; he irritated those who saw in him the apostle of dissonance, of the percussion instruments, and of lush new tone colors. (This was approximately the time when various people, some real composers, more often unconscious charlatans, were experimenting with funny noises and the description of things mechanical. Pieces like Honneger's PACIFIC 231, Antheil's BALLET MÉCANIQUE and Mossolov's (not Molotov's) IRON FOUNDRY were typical examples.)

Despite his so-called "neo-classical" twist, Stravinsky nevertheless remained the unquestionable leader of modern music in Paris and the West throughout the early 'thirties.

True enough, in the second decade of the century, another figure became powerful and highly influential, this time in the waning and neurotic central European capital of Vienna. This was Schoenberg, the great atonal father, the inventor and practitioner of a new technique of composition: the "twelve-tone system." (Usually, to a layman, these words do not mean very much, but to his ears they certainly mean a great deal. They stand for the kind of music in which conventional frontiers between dissonance and consonance are completely abolished. In this music, such a distinction seems meaningless. Everything sounds contrary to the habitual musical furnishings of our uncultivated ears and, instead of relaxing in comfortable, pretty music, we are invited to admire the supra-physical formulas of sound logistics.)

Stravinsky is primarily an artisan, a craftsman, while Schoenberg is a dogmatician, a theorist. Neither likes the other. And yet in the opinion of most musicians, both share the pontifical glories of our state of music. Since the death of Manuel de Falla and Bela Bartok, Stravinsky and Schoenberg remain the lonely "founding fathers" of this strangely eccentric and highly anarchic state. To that anarchy, in which everyone seems to go his own way, they offer a certain amount of cohesion, a certain ideological meaning.

Curiously enough, as if to fulfill a fateful anachronism, both have found refuge in Hollywood, where a true eccentric looks like a sedate Baltic burgher and anarchy is a form of matrimony.

134

It was a little past noon on December 22nd when Balanchine's wife Maria stopped the car on an incline of winding North Wetherly Drive. On our right a low white picket fence was concealed by a wall of tall evergreen shrubbery. Some two-hundred and fifty feet behind the shrubbery, silhouetted against blue-brownish hills, stood a small and flat one-story house, rimmed by a narrow porch in front and a large terrace on its left-hand side.

Balanchine climbed out of the car. "Here we are," he said, helping me to get my bags and packages out of the back seat.

From behind the shrubbery we heard hasty footsteps and Russian voices. A minute later both Stravinskys appeared at a small side gate near the garage. They were dressed in break-fast clothes — she in an impeccably white négligé, which made her look large and stately, he, in a polka-dotted burgundy bathrobe, with the striking addition of a narrow-brimmed, wilted, black felt hat. Both of them smiled and gesticulated. We all began embracing.

"*Noo, priyekhali,*" (Well, finally you've arrived) said Vera Arturovna.

"*N-da . . . enfin,*" echoed Stravinsky under his hat.

This vision made me suddenly aware of their extraordinary physical disproportion. There was something both touching and amusing in it. The tall, Olympian figure of Vera Arturovna, her broad and regular Scandinavian features, her wide-open and languidly smiling blue eyes, in such contrast to her husband's sharp facial contours, his beak-like nose and fleshy lips, and his short, totally fat-less body, so surprisingly young, so agile and elastic.

I remembered that Tchelitchew called him a "prancing grasshopper" and that Cocteau used to remark when Stravinsky conducted that he looked like "an ant acting its part in a LaFontaine fable." There is, in effect, something crickety, something insectal about the movement of his body. They are swift, precise and always well controlled, like the movements of an accomplished dancer or acrobat. Yet the moment I saw him in front of his garden in California, I knew that both Tchelitchew and Cocteau were wrong. He is neither a grasshopper not an ant; he is not an insect at all; he is much more like a bird, one of those small birds with large, sturdy beaks, like cardinals or lovebirds, whose movements are quick, electric and nervous.

"Give this to me," said Stravinsky picking up my bag. "Heavens, what is in it? Someone's meat?"

"It's only music," I replied, "and a couple of bottles."

"Ah, you brought my scores. Good for you. Only . . . you know, I don't need them anymore. I mean the Handel operas. I found most of them here and Hawkes promised to get me some more in London."

"Come, come," said Vera Arturovna, "Let's go in."

We went through the gate and walked up to the house. The path led up hill through a patch of garden banked on

136

3

one side by bushes, on the other by a few long-stemmed pink and cream-colored roses.

"Go to your right, *through* the living room," said Vera Arturovna as we reached the small entrance hall of the house. I crossed a spacious, sunny room filled with flowers, modern pictures, light colored furniture and several bird cages, and entered a smaller room, lined on two sides with bookcases. Across the room, turning its back to the terrace window, stood "the sofa."

Vera Arturovna ordered me to take off my shoes.

"The first thing we do," she said, "is to measure the prospective sleepers."

"Here they are, all of them," said Stravinsky, and he pointed to an array of marks and signatures written in pencil on different levels of the door frame.

"See, this is tiny Mrs. Bolm. She was the smallest of them all. And this is Olson, the tallest."

We started deciphering signatures.

"And who is this?" asked Maria Balanchine.

"This . . . Vera, who is this? — Ah, yes, it's Elsie Rieti."

They were both relieved when my watermark did not exceed Auden's six feet.

"Oh," said Vera Arturovna in a disappointed tone, "I thought you were much taller than Auden."

"It's only his hair," commented Stravinsky. "Come here. Stretch out on the sofa. You see," he turned to George Balanchine, "he fits perfectly: from socks to hair. Like a violin in its case."

The Balanchines were leaving to visit Maria's family. They planned to pick us all up in the evening for dinner at the Napoli, Stravinsky's Italian *stammstube*.

"I suppose you want to bathe and change," said Vera Arturovna.

"Why, he looks clean," said Igor, *"et il ne sent pas trop mauvais."*

"Noo, poydem, Igor; let's leave him alone." She dragged him by the sleeve. "When you're ready, we'll eat lunch."

"But I must show him where to wash," said Stravinsky and led me to the bathroom. Just before opening the door he turned to me and hugged me, his eyes full of pleasure and warmth. "I am really glad, Nika, that you finally came," he said. "I have so much to talk to you about and I want to see your new music."

He opened the door and let me into a small bathroom with a large black sink and a modern shower.

"This is my shower room. I hope you don't mind taking showers. I will use the other bathroom while you're here, so make yourself at home."

He closed the door carefully after having shown me how to operate the lock, the light and the shower door.

I had barely finished washing and changing when I heard him return and knock at the door.

138

"Nika, if you're ready, come out and have a drink. I have just received two bottles of Marc from a farmer in Brittany. Let's have some."

We went through a short corridor to the living room. Just before entering it, he stopped in front of a small built-in cupboard and opened the doors.

"You see, this is my cellar. I have a few remarkable bottles here; both wines and brandies. What would you like to drink for lunch? What about a Mouton Rotschild 1937? I only have a few bottles left and it's a unique wine."

Stravinsky got out a bottle of Marc and carefully extracted its cork with one of those double-decker silent French corkscrews which make one think of obstetrical instruments. Having accomplished the operation, he fondly smelled the cork and looking very earnest said, *"N-da,* this is perfectly reliable Marc," and added in English, "Not so bad!"

We gulped the Marc, Stravinsky making a smacking sound with his tongue.

"Now, quickly, some proteins! Verotchka, where are the proteins?" he shouted excitedly. "Give Nabokov and me some proteins."

"Ah, here they are," he said as we entered the living room. He gave me a plate-full of biscuits thickly smeared with camembert cheese.

The lunch tasted good after three days of Pullman cooking. The small and narrow dining room was lit by a northern bay window hung with long white tulle curtains. The pale light gave the entire room an atmosphere of neatness and airy coolness.

Before we sat down, Stravinsky repeated the cork-extraction ceremony, this time with more ritualistic concentration and a greater amount of cork-smelling, tongue-smacking and a more emphatic, "Not so bad."

During lunch they asked me all sorts of questions, mostly concerning the political situation. I had quite recently returned from Berlin after two years with the U. S. Military Government. This, coupled with a general interest in politics, made me, in their eyes, an expert analyst of any political situation. Furthermore, as I undoubtedly had acquaintance with government secrets, I surely would be able to predict the course of world events.

The main question was whether there would be another war and consequently whether it would be safe to plan a European tour for the coming summer months. There was real anxiety in the way Stravinsky asked this question several times during the meal. I was of course aware of his profound distaste for any form of social upheaval, be it a war, a revolution, a strike, or simply a mild political demonstration. "How can one work in disorder?" he would say.

His former publisher, Gabriel Païtchadze, once described to me how perplexed and jittery he became when he was caught in Paris at the outbreak of the war. He could neither eat nor sleep, he could not work; an occasional bomb-blast made him jumpy; he got angry, nervous and irritable. All he wanted was to get out as quickly as possible, out of Paris, out of Europe, into America where life was still orderly.

I remembered his departing remark to a mutual friend, shortly after Pearl Harbor, at the time when communication between the continents was non-existent. Unable to keep in touch with his family and friends, Stravinsky felt very sharply the general war anxiety. On his way back to Hollywood after a tour in the east, he had had dinner with a few close friends. During dinner the conversation had apparently been of a concentrated gloom. As he was leaving, Stravinsky took my friend aside on the platform at Grand Central Station and asked him in a low, halting whisper:

"Tell me, quite unequivocally, will there be a revolution in America, or not?"

My friend squirmed, wavered and answered.

"How can I know? . . . Maybe, maybe not . . ."

"But where will I go if there is one?" said Stravinsky in an appalled and indignant tone.

For Stravinsky social disorder of *any* kind is primarily something which prevents him from doing his work — that is, fulfilling his duty. He hates it with all the strength of his egocentric nature. He dislikes even the terms *revolution* or *revolutionary*, particularly when they are applied to music. He is very angry when music historians use them (for example

141

in sentences like: "The early *revolutionary* works of Stravinsky . . ." or "The *revolutionary* discoveries of Beethoven's immortal genius which swept etc. . . ." or somewhat Freudian and up-to-date: "The *revolutionary* recognition of tonality as a traumatic condition.") "What can they possibly mean?" he says. "Revolution is a term describing the overthrow of an existing order by means of violence. It is necessarily accompanied by disorder. Music is the antithesis of violence and disorder. Music is order, measure, proportion, that is, all those principles which oppose disorder. The only thing this term can mean is a cycle, a span of time," and with a didactic emphasis on each word he adds, "This is the only *correct* way to use it."

Stravinsky is equally fearful and contemptuous of conditions in which the creative work of the artist is subject to supervision or dictation (and possibly extinction) by the authorities of the state.

"Tell me please," he would say with intense irritation, "what can these gentlemen (the authorities) know about how to write music? I don't try and tell them how to be a *tchinovnik* (a bureaucrat)."

Hence Stravinsky's deep disgust for the situation of the artist in the Soviet Union, "where every *tchinovnik* can tell you what to do."

"I ask you," he says, "what is the difference between conditions today and the time of Glinka, when Nicholas I had to approve the libretto of *The Life for the Tzar* before the music was written? At least Nicholas did not try to tell Glinka what kind of music to write."

"No, my friend," he would say, lifting his shoulders and grinning sardonically, "let them stew in their own juice. I don't want anything to do with it. Let them make their music à la Mr. Syerov and others of his ilk."

Stravinsky usually follows up such a tirade with one of his most typical remarks in Russian: *"Noo, komoo èto noozhno:* who, after all, needs all this?"

Hence also his spontaneous and sincere attachment to the United States, where he can work in peace, earn a comfortable income and feel secure and happy.

"America is good for me," he often says. "He has become softer and is less frequently angry," echoes his wife.

Stravinsky does not permit criticism of America in his presence. He usually interrupts and changes the conversation or, in an aside, says, "As far as I am concerned, they can have their Marshals and Fuehrers. Leave me Mr. Truman and I'm quite satisfied."

After lunch, in the living room, Vera Arturovna introduced me to the lesser (only in size, not in affectionate standing) members of the household.

"Here is Pópka," she said, taking a small grey parrot out of a cage and seating him on her husband's shoulder. "He is two years old. Did you see his picture in *Time* magazine? He usually eats with us at the table when we are alone."

"Look, Vera, look!" interrupted Igor Fedorovitch as the parrot flew toward me, landed on my shoulder and began climbing on top of my head. "He is already flirting with Nabokov. *C'est un grand amoureux.*"

"It's Nika's mane," said Vera Arturovna. "You're a Mélisande for him."

"Pópka is after vermin and lice and not after Mélisande," remarked Stravinsky caustically, and he added, "Be careful; you know what birds do on people's heads."

Besides the parrot, the feathered household consists of a weather-beaten and henpecked-looking canary, whose name is *Lyssaya Dushka* (Bold Darling), and a flock of about eight love birds.

Bold Darling and Pópka are friends. The parrot opens the canary's cage, lets it out and both fly around in circles in the living room. Stravinsky likes the parrot and the canary but is quite indifferent to the lovebirds. Hence Dushka's and Pópka's cages stand in the living room, each near a window. Opposite a large white mantelpiece, as if to tease them, hang several engravings of falcons, eagles and other birds of prey with large protruding beaks.

The lovebirds' cage stands outdoors on the porch. Vera Arturovna took me there to see them. As we were examining them, she told me their names.

144

"These are Beauty and Pretty," she said showing me two pale-blue birds seated tightly together on the upper rung of the large cage. "They were the first — given to us by Emil Ludwig. And this one here with her sexy eyes is Lana Turner; near her is her youngest brother or lover, 'Whit-Whit.' They all inter-married and now it's one happy incestuous family."

She turned away from the cage and pointed at a big black cat stretched out in the sun. "And this is our only quadruped — Vasska. His fully name is Vassily Vassilyevitch Lechkin: he was described in the *New Yorker* and also in *Time*. When I used to run a picture gallery, I always sent him a printed invitation and wrote on it: 'Please do come: — fishbones, cocktails.'"

Stravinsky appeared on the terrace and called me. "Nika, if you aren't too tired, come and show me your music."

"But Igor, let him rest," said Vera Arturovna. "You must be tired. Why don't you take a nap till tea-time?"

I said I wasn't tired. I wanted very much to go to his study.

"Perhaps I could show you my music some other time," I said. "Now I would rather look at your ORPHEUS."

I I I

"All right, come with me," said Stravinsky. He led me to his study at the other end of the narrow corridor, where we had had a drink before lunch.

He sat down at the piano, carefully wiped his glasses with Sight Savers and opened the orchestra score of ORPHEUS. A moment later we were both absorbed in it.

I stood behind him and watched the short, nervous fingers scour the keyboard, searching and finding the correct intervals, the widely-spaced chords and the characteristically Stravinskyan broad melodic leaps. His neck, his head, his whole body accentuated the ingenious rhythmical design of the music by spasm-like bobs and jerks. He grunted, he hummed, and occasionally stopped to make an aside.

"See the fugue here," he would say, pointing to the beginning of the Epilogue. "The two horns are working it out, while a trumpet and a violin in unison sing a long, drawn-out melody, a kind of *cantus firmus*. Doesn't this melody sound to you like a medieval *vièle* (a viol)? Listen . . ." And his fingers would start fidgeting again on the keyboard. Then, coming to a passage in the Epilogue where a harp solo interrupts the slow progress of the fugue, he would stop and say: "Here, you see, I cut off the fugue with a pair of scissors." He clipped the air with his fingers. "I introduced this short harp phrase, like two bars of an accompaniment. Then the horns go on with their fugue as if nothing had happened. I repeat it at regular intervals, here and here again." Stravinsky added, with his habitual grin, "You can eliminate these harp-solo interruptions, paste the parts of the fugue together and it will be one whole piece."

I asked him why did he introduce the harp solo. "What's the point of cutting up the fugue this way?" I said.

He smiled maliciously as if he were introducing me to one of his private secrets. "But didn't you hear? The harp solo is

146

taken from another section." He turned the pages to the middle of the score. "It is a reminder of the Song of Orpheus." And he added thoughtfully: "Here in the Epilogue it sounds like a kind of . . . compulsion, like something unable to stop . . . Orpheus is dead, the song is gone, but the accompaniment goes on."

In this Epilogue, Stravinsky once again, reveals his uncanny sense of the individuality or, better, the personality of each instrument of the orchestra. It is this sense which enables him not only to find for each dramatic situation (when he is concerned with a dramatic subject) the most suitable and therefore the most expressive instrumental combination, but also each time to discover a new and surprisingly fresh mixture of orchestral sound. All this, as I said before, is accomplished with the greatest economy of means (few polyphonic lines, a minimum of tones in chords, a minimum of instruments to each melodic line) and the most astute use of the specific qualities of each instrument. Stravinsky is, I believe, unquestionably the greatest living investigator of instruments as *individuals,* perhaps even the greatest since the middle of the 18th Century.

The experimentation with instruments in the 19th Century was primarily concerned with the extension of their range and their dynamic power. The specific expressive qualities of each individual instrument was a secondary consideration. The motive was not a craftsmanlike interest in the technical possibilities of each instrument but the need of finding the neces-

147

sary so-called "tone-colors" on the orchestral palette, in order to suggest or describe the extra-musical images, expressions, ideas or objects with which romantic music was pre-occupied. Only towards the end of that century did composers show a renewed concern with instruments as individuals within the orchestral unit. Previous to this time, instruments were constantly added to the symphony orchestra. The orchestra devoured them with an ogre's appetite and grew bigger and fatter in volume. The individuality of each instrument, however, was being drowned out by the mammoth sound, by impersonal mixtures of this newly-invented engine of musical warfare — the 100-piece symphony orchestra.

In retrospect, this "development" added little to musical culture. The new symphony orchestra was a delight to those who like to bathe in a sea of mushy sound, and of course a delight to the orchestra conductor, but it was an abomination to all those who cared for clarity, precision and transparency in the art of music.

Naturally there were exceptional composers who continued to be interested in the individuality or personality of musical instruments, such as Tchaikowsky (mainly in his ballet scores) or Verdi or even, at times, Richard Wagner, normally the greatest offender against the mores of the individual instrument, and above all Debussy.

Today, in the middle of the 20th Century, the attitude of the composers towards the instruments of the orchestra, and hence to the art of orchestration, has definitely changed. Composers know that *orchestration* is not *registration* (not like pulling the stops on a huge electric organ in order to acquire impersonal and phony mixtures of sound), but that it is rather a highly complex art, in which the intuitive or imaginative faculties of the composer's mind are combined with the logical and critical faculties. Thus, this art can be completely successful only when the composer thoroughly understands the individuality of each instrument in the orchestra. On this knowledge he must base his own art of orchestration.

This does not mean, as people often think, that the composer should be able to play most of the instruments of the orchestra. His is a different ability than that of the performing artist; the ability to perform has little to do with the composer's work; it may even sometimes be a handicap; that is, it may lead the composer to estimate the possibilities of the instruments by his own standards of performance. This will inevitably result in a timorous and bland orchestration.

The primary importance the art of orchestration holds today in contemporary music is largely due to the influence of Stravinsky. If we consider that at least two-thirds of the quality of an instrumental piece is in its adequate orchestration, we must give credit to Stravinsky's approach to and his discoveries in the instrumental field.

His approach is essentially based on his knowledge of the technical possibilities of each instrument. Hence his imaginative and extremely skillful exploitation of these possibilities. In other words, Stravinsky treats every orchestra musician as an accomplished performer, a master craftsman of his instrument. He requires of him the ability to play at high velocity and at the same time to feel at ease in a complex rhythmical design; he must be able to intone with mathematical precision in all the ranges of his instrument and at all possible dynamic conditions of the music (from very soft to very loud) and, finally, he must strive to extend the ranges of his instrument beyond the conventionally accepted limits.

This by no means implies that Stravinsky expects the impossible from instrumentalists in the orchestra. Rather the opposite is true — in most of his scores, particularly in the last twenty years — the writing for instruments is fairly simple and hence not too difficult to perform. "It is for the conductor that I make things difficult," says Stravinsky. "It is to him that I make my demands."

This is why modern minded orchestra musicians like to play Stravinsky. When you ask them if they like his music, they usually reply that they do, because it is *interestingly* written for their particular instrument.

Thus by using unexploited registers of instruments, by discovering new technical devices, by employing certain instruments to perform melodic outlines usually associated with other instruments, or by combining instrumental sounds that are considered unsound and unorthodox by the orchestral canons of the 19th Century (according to the treatises on orchestration by such pundits as Berlioz, Richard Strauss and Rimsky-Korsakoff), Igor Stravinsky achieves an incredible variety of orchestral combinations which always sound new, fresh and, at the same time, persuasive. In these last twenty-five or thirty years, the orchestral texture of his music has acquired a degree of transparency, lucidity and crystalline fragility unequalled by any of his contemporaries. At times, it is a kind of orchestral tight-rope walking, precarious and precise . . . Diaghilev once remarked to me while we were listening to a new work of Stravinsky's (I believe it was the OCTET for Wind Instruments), that it was so transparent, that "one could see through it with one's ears."

Stravinsky and I spent most of the afternoon looking at the score of ORPHEUS and at the two parts of the Latin MASS he was writing at the time.

After awhile I grew tired of standing and flopped down on a soft, narrow couch that stood behind the piano in his study. On one side of its dark silk surface lay a neatly folded plaid rug, and on the other a dainty and immaculately white little pillow. By then, Stravinsky had entirely forgotten my presence and was absorbed in one of the pages of his Mass. He was playing the same passage over and over again. It looked as if he were probing or, rather, testing the quality of what he had written. He was re-measuring the interval relations and re-calculating the rhythmical patterns. His head and body jerked and bobbed as before and he was quite distinctly humming the words of the Mass.

I suddenly caught myself following his movements with a special kind of interest. Often before I had been captivated by the movements of his body. They are always so personal and profoundly revealing of his personality and of his music. Frequently, in fact, while listening to his music, I have closed my eyes and heard or rather seen in front of me a characteristic Stravinskyan gesture. At other times when seeing him pace the floor on tip-toes, in the middle of a discussion his upper body bent forward like that of a frog-fishing stork, his arms akimbo, I would be struck by the parallel between his physical gesture and the inner gesture of his music. His music reflects his peculiarly elastic walk, the syncopated nod of his head and shrug of his shoulders, and those abrupt stops in the middle of a conversation when, like a dancer, he suddenly freezes in a ballet-like pose and punctuates his argument with a broad and sarcastic grin.

But not only does Stravinsky's music reflect his bodily movements and characteristic gestures; it also reflects succinctly and convincingly his whole mode of life — his attitude towards his environment, towards people, nature and objects. Above all, it reflects his love for order and his meticulously stern work discipline, so totally devoid of self-indulgence and self-pity. It reflects his penchant for all sorts of mechanical gadgets, from

152

thumbtacks to stop watches and pocket metronomes, his passion for hardware stores and the pleasure he derives from fitting a message into the prescribed twenty-five words of an overnight cable. (On December 23rd, we spent nearly an hour at the Western Union office while he "tailored," as he called it, two Christmas cables to his sons.) It reflects his attitude towards money, for which, as everybody knows, he has a "profound respect," which some people mistake for avarice.

Sometimes he makes amusing comparisons between music and money. For example, once during one of his habitual bitter attacks against contemporary composers, he said, "Why they've lost all sense of the interval. They don't hear intervals and have no respect for them. One should treat intervals as if they were dollars."

But perhaps, in an even stranger way, his music reflects his nervous and acid hates; his hate of all kinds of stupidity (stupid people, stupid art, stupid letters), his hate of stuffy rooms, of dirt, or disorder, of dusty furniture and bad odors. The wittiness of his caustic remarks about people and, chiefly, about bad music, is the same kind of wit one finds in some of his scores, in, for example, his ballet JEUX DE CARTES or the dances from his HISTOIRE DU SOLDAT, or his ballet RENARD. It is a scathing, pitiless kind of humor which knows no compassion. He will often, for example, distort the name of a person or a piece of music he dislikes (usually because the person or the

153

piece of music is a bore), or else he will invent a funny nickname for it. Thus Richard Strauss' ROSENKAVALIER is usually called the "Sklerosenkavalier," and the music of Shostakovitch is an "old oyster." (This is derived from an article of mine on Shostakovitch in which I compared the flabby structure of his antediluvial symphonies to that of an oyster. Stravinsky loved this comparison and at the time wrote me a warm congratulatory letter.)

In general, Stravinsky likes precise, picturesque or onomatopoëtic remarks. His talk as well as his letters are full of them. Once in New York a cold bothered him. He complained: *"J'ai un porte-monnaie dans ma nossoglotka"* (I have a purse in my larynx). Another time we were discussing his new opera, THE RAKE'S PROGRESS. He was explaining how he intended to treat Auden's libretto: "I will lace each aria with a tight corset."

People often irritate him when they stop him in a store or on a street corner and ask him, "Excuse me, aren't you the composer of the FIREBIRD?" after which they produce an autograph book. "You know," he says, "I'll hire a secretary and call him Mr. Firebird, and when people ask me this I will be able to say, 'Oh, no, *this* is Mr. Firebird — in person, flesh and bone.'"

Stravinsky's love for clear terms, for laconic definitions and adequate translation manifests itself in his enthusiasm for dictionaries, with which his study is filled. Of all of them he prefers the French "Grand Larousse."

154

"You know what sex is?" he would ask, opening the Larousse. "Listen: *le sex est une conformation particulière de l'être vivant, qui lui assigne un rôle spécial dans l'acte de généraration.* (The sexual organ is a formation peculiar to living beings, who delegate to it a special role in the act of procreation.) Isn't this a superb definition?"

His own remarks generally have a Laroussian precision as well as wit and imagination. When, for example, someone is in a hurry, he will say, "why do you hurry? *I have no time to hurry.*" But particularly sharp and picturesque are his remarks about people. An overly emotional conductor, who bristles with exuberant gestures, reminds him of a *"danse du ventre vu par derrière"* (an oriental belly dancer seen from behind), while his arms are a pair of "eggbeaters."

Conductors in general readily incur Stravinsky's wrath and his most scathing remarks. In a filing cabinet under his piano, in a separate folder, are collected some choice pictures of conductors in highly contorted poses. Most of these pictures are taken from publicity releases or newspapers.

"Look at him!" says Stravinsky, pulling a conductorial extravaganza out of the folder. "Look at the dandy! Look at his idiotic expression, his frothy gestures. Is all this nonsense necessary to conduct an orchestra?"

His workroom is another example of the precision which orders his music and his language. An extraordinary room, perhaps the best planned and organized workroom I have seen in my life. In a space which is not larger than some

155

twenty by thirty feet stand two pianos (one grand, one upright), two desks (a small, elegant writing desk and a draughtsman's table). In two cupboards with glass shelves are books, scores and sheet music, arranged according to alphabetical order. Between the two pianos, the cupboards and desks are scattered a few small tables (one of which is a kind of "smoker's delight": it exhibits all sorts of cigaret boxes, lighters, holders, fluids, flints and pipe-cleaners), five or six comfortable chairs and the couch Stravinsky uses for his afternoon naps. (I saw him on it the next day, lying on his back, with an expression of contained anger on his face, snoring gently and methodically.)

Besides the pianos and the furniture, there are hundreds of gadgets, photographs, trinkets and implements of every kind in and on the desks and tables and tacked on the back of the cupboards. I believe Stravinsky has in his study all the instruments needed for writing, copying, drawing, pasting, cutting, clipping, filing, sharpening and glueing that the combined effects of a stationery and hardware store can furnish (and yet he is always after new ones). A touch of nature in the midst of all this man-made gadgetry is provided by a bunch of fresh roses in a white china vase which stands on his desk. His wife cuts them for him every morning from his special rose bushes.

Yet despite this mass of objects and cluster of furniture, Stravinsky's study is so well organized and so functional that it gives one a sense of spaciousness and peaceful comfort. One feels as if one were surveying a chessboard, with its black and white figures arranged in exact relation to each other, ready for a long, musical game.

At the same time the room seems as compact as an antheap. When its owner moves cagily through the little corridors formed by the various pieces of furniture, he gives the impression of a busy and diligent ant crawling through the orderly labyrinth of his citadel. In fact, Stravinsky's own attitude towards his study is very much like that of an ant. He loves to carry objects of all kinds into his study. If someone brings him a present, as I was able to observe on Christmas day, he will not open it in front of his wife, or anyone else. He will wait for a convenient moment and then quietly slip away with it to his study. There he will unwrap it and, if he likes it or it appears useful, he will find a niche for it among his other souvenirs and gadgets . . .

While I was still sitting on the couch and Stravinsky was puttering at the piano, Vera Arturovna appeared in the entrance to the study and announced that the Balanchines had arrived.

"George and Maria are here," she said, "and Genia Berman is waiting for us with vodka and *zakousska* (horsd'oevres). It is time to go, Igor. Come, Nika."

"*Seytchas, seytchas,*" answered Stravinsky.

I got up to join her while Stravinsky, without changing

his position at the piano, said to me, "Nika, please go and tell them that I'll be out in five minutes." And he went on playing.

Half an hour later we were driving down to Eugene Berman's apartment. On the front seat of the car, squeezed in between Vera Arturovna and myself, was Stravinsky's tiny figure, dressed in a peajacket and a yachtsman's hat. (He bought the peajacket at a Navy surplus sale and is both proud and fond of it.) The Balanchines followed us closely in their own car.

Eugene Berman, the painter, is one of the few members of Stravinsky's Hollywood "family circle." A gentle, soft-spoken and somewhat melancholic man with a wistful sense of humor, Berman is devoted to the Stravinskys and they in turn to him. While I was in Hollywood, Berman came nearly every afternoon to the Stravinskys, stayed for meals and long into the night. One felt that Vera Arturovna and Igor Fedoro-vitch with their warm and attentive friendship, had made their house a home for Berman.

We entered the hall of Berman's apartment house and went to the desk. Vera Arturovna announced our arrival. The telephone operator, an elderly lady with glasses and a light hue of whiskers, looked at Stravinsky and, recognizing him in his nautical apparel, said, "Aren't you the author of . . . Firebird?"

"You see?" whispered Stravinsky. "It never fails."

He smiled charmingly and answered, "Yes, madam, Firebird is a bird of mine."

The dinner at Napoli was gay and happy, like one of those dinners of the 'twenties when we used to get together with Diaghilev, Prokofiev, Picasso, Derain, Balanchine and other collaborators of the Ballet Russe at Giardini's restaurant on the top of the hill in Monte Carlo.

Stravinsky was in wonderful form — voluble, witty and, at the same time, extremely attentive to all of us. As usual, he ordered the best food and, especially, the best wines, and he had the waiter play funny, sobbing, old Caruso records on the juke box.

But gay and happy as the occasion was, both Balanchine and I couldn't keep from yawning — so much so that Vera Arturovna and her husband (who usually can sit it out till the early hours of the morning, provided he is with close friends and there is Scotch around) started to urge us all to go to bed as soon as we had finished coffee.

But by the time we came home and I fitted myself comfortably on the three cushions of the famous sofa, my tiredness was gone and I felt just as wide awake as when I had arrived that morning at the Los Angeles station. I looked around for books and found a few rare Russian editions on a shelf that contained a pell-mell assortment of French novels, Russian classics, murder stories and biographies. There were no books on music except Mozart's "Letters." Among the books were the epigrammatic works of that peculiar and quite unjustly forgotten Russian thinker and writer of the beginning of this century, Rozanov (whom I knew Stravinsky liked very much and whose works he re-reads and quotes constantly, comparing Rozanov's ideas and style to Gogol and Dostoevsky). I took down a volume of Rozanov called "Fallen Leaves" and tried to read but soon discovered that I could not concentrate and that my eyes were wandering senselessly over and over the same sentences. I was still too much under the influence of my afternoon with Stravinsky in his study and all my thoughts were concerned with his work. Somehow I felt that I had to find answers all over again to essential questions about his art.

What, after all, does his art mean to us contemporary musicians of the younger generation? What is its value in the general evolution of music history? What are his essential discoveries?

It is difficult to say something new about Stravinsky's music. All seems to have been said. There has rarely been a composer whose work has been as much discussed during his lifetime than the work of Stravinsky. He, himself, in his two books — his "Autobiography" and his "Poetics of Music" — has stated his point of view on the art of music and thus by inference discussed his own art. Everything one says seems redundant and commonplace.

And yet, lying on his sofa in his house, surrounded by his

warm friendliness, I felt overcome by an enormous sense of gratefulness for his art, the kind of gratefulness an apprentice feels towards his master craftsman. I felt that I owed Stravinsky much of my understanding of how to use the materials of music — intervals, rhythms, melodic outlines. I felt that it was his art that opened my eyes to the decay of impressinist harmony and the corruption or the emotive paroxysms of late Romanticism. Above all I felt that it was his example that had brought me to admire the continuity of the classical tradition, the beauty of polyphonic technique, and to understand the necessity for a clear-cut, well-defined formal structure.

At the same time it was Stravinsky's art, I believe, which showed the musicians of my generation new horizons in the domain of rhythm, new possibilities in the use of musical instruments and a new concept of Harmony, fuller, broader and nobler than the sterile harmonic concepts of the late 19th Century. Yet to me the most important discoveries of Stravinsky lie in his approach to the problem of musical time or, better, in his artful perception and measurement of the flow of time by means of the most complex and beautiful rhythmic patterns and designs.

Who else, I thought, among contemporary composers can exhibit such a continuity and such a variety of admirable works of art (or should I say solutions of "problems")? Who else has *successfully* used *all* forms, *all* styles, *all* techniques and integrated them in an unmistakably personal art of his own?

Who else in our time has written pieces so easily understood and of such immense popular appeal to the layman, like "The Firebird," "Petrushka," "Histoire du Soldat," (in the 'twenties in Central Europe thousands of schools performed this piece to the general delight of teen-agers. My own son, when he was about seven, loved this piece more than anything else and always wanted me to play the records of it over and over again), SYMPHONY OF PSALMS and APOLLO and at the same time has produced such hermetic masterpieces as the SYMPHONY and OCTET for Wind Instruments, or the SERENADE for piano solo (which is the joy of a skilled music-lover). And finally how few, how very few composers of our time can produce a record of such total devotion to his craft, so completely devoid of any concession or compromise, so intransigent and conscientious.

When . . .

I was suddenly interrupted in the middle of my thoughts by soft footsteps in the living room. The door opened and Stravinsky appeared, in his bathrobe.

"Why aren't you sleeping? Put the light out. It's late," he said reproachfully. He walked over to the window. "Don't open it so wide — especially with your neuralgia. Our California nights aren't warm at all." And having shut the window to a small crack, he left.

IV

The days in California went by much faster than I would

have wished. The weather was exceptionally sunny and warm, even for old Hollywooders like the Stravinskys. The soft, gentle air, the roses and carnations in the garden, the accumulation of neat, fancy-colored packages in the living room and the deluge of Christmas cards on the mantlepiece; all of this made me feel happy and carefree. They brought back holiday memories of my childhood: the smells of the French Riviera, the lilac-colored sea of Yalta and the tuberoses in my mother's room one Easter morning in Odessa. In fact, this Hollywood holiday seemed more like Easter than Christmas.

The days were filled with music, talk, enjoyment and gayety. I had rarely seen Stravinsky so gay and so full of fun. Balanchine was right. He did not leave me for an instant. He upset his normally rigid work schedule to spend all his time with Balanchine and me. We would go marketing and Christmas shopping. He helped me choose one of those artsy-craftsy silver bracelets for my wife. (When the salesgirl brought out a tray filled with all sorts of silver jewelry, I said to Stravinsky, "What should I buy?" "First of all," he answered sententiously, "I must know how much money you are ready to assign to this purchase.")

One afternoon they took me to the ocean via the interminable Sunset Boulevard, where I was to "salute" the Pacific by dipping my finger into its waters. In doing so I got my feet wet and was ordered to take off my shoes, for fear of a cold. Another day they drove me all around the avenues and hills of Hollywood, past those curious blue, pink and silver Christmas trees which stand on its street corners and in gas stations.

We went several times to the lunch market to have lunch with the Aldous Huxleys and a few other friends, and I got lost in the maze of Italian, French and Spanish food counters.

One entire evening was spent listening to the Toscanini records of LA TRAVIATA, which N.B.C. made especially for Stravinsky, at his request, (of Verdi's operas, Stravinsky likes LA TRAVIATA and AIDA best of all; he is less fond of OTHELLO and FALSTAFF) and the Glyndebourne recordings of DON GIOVANNI. This opera is Stravinsky's special love; particularly now that he himself is busy writing an opera.

"Listen to the length of those lines," he would say. "Listen how clever they are, *quel souffle, quelle clarté!*"

On Christmas morning Stravinsky, at my request, exhibited his Hungarian calisthenics. Not knowing anything about gymnastic exercises, I was unable to see how they differed from the usual calisthenics or the German "Dr. Mueller's *Koerperliche Morgenauffrischŭngs-ŭebŭngen*" (Dr. Mueller's bodily morning refresher exercises), which were popular in Russia during my childhood. It seemed to me, however, that some of the exercises had a kind of Turkish or Magyar flavor, perhaps because Stravinsky when doing them rolled his eyes like a dervish in a trance.

164

The calisthenics were interrupted by the doorbell. Stravinsky, who was in bathing trunks, ran to his room to dress. I opened the door to a middle-aged gentleman with a Christmas present in his hand.

"I'd like to see Mr. Stravinsky," said the gentleman, pronouncing the name Straw-windsky. "I'm from the X. Blueprinting Company."

When Stravinsky appeared, the gentleman took off his hat and wished Stravinsky "a very merry Christmas." And he added, "And here's a little token of our appreciation."

Stravinsky thanked him politely and ceremoniously and took the present. The gentleman put on his hat and said, "Why don't you open it right here, Mr. Straw-windsky."

Stravinsky unwrapped the gift, which appeared to be one of those commercial calendars with semi-nude teasers on each page.

"How d'you like our calendar?" said the gentleman with a wink.

Stravinsky shook his head in approval. "Very nice, very nice. Thank you very much."

"Wait a minute," said the gentleman. "Turn to April."

Stravinsky turned to April.

"How d'you like *that* gal?"

"Very pretty, very nice young lady," replied Stravinsky.

"Now take a look at October and tell me what you think

of *that*," said the gentleman, taking the calendar out of Stravinsky's hand and proudly exposing to our view a pair of succulent, cream-colored female buttocks.

"Very good, very true to life," said Stravinsky, with even greater sobriety.

At this, the man approached Stravinsky, tweaked his left ear-lobe, and with a club-man's smile said, "You rascal!" After he had gone, Stravinsky roared with laughter and shouted, "Vera, Vera! look what I've received."

That same evening the small circle of Stravinsky's family and friends gathered at his house for a Christmas party. There were just a few people: Stravinsky's daughter and her French husband, the two Bolms — the famous dancer and his tiny wife — Eugene Berman and Stravinsky's physician, Dr. Edel, with his broad Austrian accent and equally broad, friendly smile, and, finally, the two Balanchines. We all had a quiet and happy dinner with lots of wine and each of us received a carefully "premeditated" present (Balanchine and I had silver goblets for drinking vodka). During dinner the conversation, out of deference to Maria Balanchine, lingered in a kind of pigeon English, but after dinner and late into the night the linguistic wind blew stronger and stronger in the Russian direction, to the mutual disappointment of Maria Balanchine, Dr. Edel and Stravinsky's French son-in-law.

The next day, December 26th, I had to go back to New York. We drove to the airport through the darkening hours

166

of the evening, long in advance of take-off time (an old Russian custom). At the TWA counter we were told that the plane was one hour late and that all planes in the East were grounded or delayed. (It was the day after the big snow storm in New York.) I somehow hoped that the plane would not take off and that I could go back with them to North Wetherly Drive.

We sat in the waiting room unnoticed by anyone. A fat man passed by and went to the traffic counter.

"You know who that is?" said Vera Arturovna. "It's Alfred Hitchcock."

"And there," added Stravinsky, "is Henry Fonda. It looks as if you're going to have lots of famous men on the plane with you."

Near the exit gate stood someone whom I thought I knew. He was dressed in one of those movie-star specials: an overly-long and broad polocoat. He was talking to a pretty woman wearing a felt hat and a cabbage-size orchid. Her face also seemed familiar. I asked Vera Arturovna who she was.

"I think it's June Havoc, the sister of the famous strip-teaser."

Finally the plane was called and we started moving towards Gate No. 2. The man in the polo coat turned to me and said, "I think we have met in Vienna. Aren't you Nicolas Nabokov? My name is Helmut Dantine."

"Oh, yes," I said. "How are you?" ("One more famous man," whispered Stravinsky.)

We parted at the gate and I walked with the crowd of

passengers through a tunnel to the plane, leaving the two Stravinskys on the platform in front of the terminal. But we were kept waiting for about twenty minutes before we could board the plane.

As I was going up the steps of the gangplank, I looked back toward the terminal. There in the bright California moonlight I saw a small figure frantically waving his hat. I waved back and entered the plane.

Helmut Dantine approached me and asked in a quaint Viennese accent, "Excuse me, who was that man with whom you came to the airport? His face looks so familiar."

I explained.

"That's what I thought," he said. "But what is he doing in Hollywood? Oh, yes, on second thought I heard that he was here. Is he doing a picture?"

I answered that he was not.

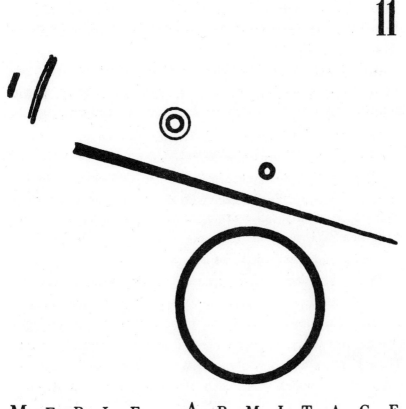

M E R L E   A R M I T A G E

1949   The Age of Stravinsky

The great parabola of Stravinsky is coming into focus. In the forty years since he burst through the barriers that separated Russia from Europe and the west, he has been the most controversial, inventive and influential of the composers, radiating forces which have extended well beyond the confines of music. Only Picasso and his influence on painting is measurably comparable.

Anthropologists of the future may be able to explain the forces released at the turn of the twentieth century which produced an artistic, scientific and engineering explosion which had been smouldering for a hundred years.

At the time, this phenomenon appeared as a series of unrelated detonations. Only now are we beginning to understand the nature of the forces which have made this fifty year period utterly different in texture, attitude, content and dimension. We now see it as one great upward surge. The individual and group destinies are fascinating.

Freud, Jung and Adler appeared and we became aware of the application of psychology and psychiatry. Sudden changes and new developments occurred in logic, chemistry, neurology, biology, psychiatry, aerodynamics and mathematics and physics. These changes and developments were either new concepts or old concepts which had taken startling turns, and dogmas which had been unquestioningly accepted for centuries were either discounted or completely upset.

To accentuate the confusion, all these newly gained perceptions were accelerated by dynamic changes in transportation and communication. Materials and products formerly the result of laborious hand-work began to emerge in speedily fabricated quantities from machines.

Everything was in rebellion.

Virile artists, sickened by the banal and sentimental state of painting, insisted upon a new beginning. Cezanne, an unrecognized giant, began to return painting to its vital purposes through the intelligent employment of color, construction and form. Others, including the unprecedented Picasso, returned to such simple shapes as the cube, the cone and the cylinder, and *cubism,* a powerful new influence, was born. Kandinsky and another group of progressives, contributed a new sense and employment of space relationships. Painting was on its way to maintain a "company front" with its fellow insurgents.

Floundering in the word-ridden Victorian swamps of formless romanticism, literature suddenly ceased to be a meaningless imitation of past glories, and responded to the galvanizing ministrations of James Joyce, Gertrude Stein, E. E. Cummings, and a host of younger writers. In expressing the ever-shifting kaleidoscopic impressions of the stream of consciousness, a new and profound dimension began to exert a healthy influence on all contemporary literature.

Into this ferment which had assumed only a tentative character and had disclosed but a fraction of its potential power, richocheted a barbaric thrust from Russia, a penetration in depth in three movements: Russian painting, Russian opera and, prophetically, Russian ballet. Europe was stunned. For the next many seasons, Diaghileff and his company created a ballet

171

fever in every European capital. Exotic Russian women and physically vital men danced before lush decors by Bakst, Anisfelt and Roerich to the music of Tschaikowsky, Rimsky-Korsakoff, Borodin, Glinka, Schumann, Debussy, and a shattering new composer, Stravinsky. Everything from painting to fashions responded to this cyclonic and hypnotising ensemble with its Byzantine overtones, and the forward movement in aesthetics temporarily gave way to the irrespressible power of organized color, movement and sound.

But out of this recession into the pagan Elysian fields and delightful sensuous experiences came the one element which was to join, revitalize, and reinforce the significant mutations of the twentieth century — the music of Stravinsky. All the rest is memorable history.

The music of Stravinsky has the anatomy of evolution, not of revolution. It may be that future historians will find that Edgar Varèse wrote the *revolutionary* music of our time, a music identified more directly with the forces of the cosmos — with an awesome power from electrical storms to exploding nebulae.

The music of Stravinsky is of infinite and astounding variety — the range from LE SACRE and LES NOCES to OCTOUR and HISTORY OF THE SOLDIER is unparalleled in the works of other composers. But it is all strung on one very tough if tenuous strand — a rare Stravinskian concept of form and structure.

172

It might be within the realm of truth to say that Stravinsky uses musical materials *once removed,* creating with elements already in one stage of creation.

With composers who have gone directly to nature, the result is often a synthesis of music and literature — a music concerned with allegory — a music freighted with human and emotional connotations. It is the wheat in its complete stock and stem brought to the threshing-machine, which eliminates the stock and stem, and pours forth a stream of grain. It is the *grain* which seems to interest Stravinsky, who carries the process further — to flour and bread and pastry, if we may use such simple parallels to illustrate such complex and profound processes of creation.

Possibly the art of Picasso can help us understand the accomplishments of Stravinsky. If a painter may be said to start with reality, which he then transmuted — then Picasso begins with forms already transmuted, which he in turn reorganizes and relates after his own convictions.

Even Stravinsky's LE SACRE DU PRINTEMPS, a work founded on the primitive rites of a physical world awakening from its winter of sleep, is already apart from commerce with the alchemy of spring — and cut off from any reality of association. It remains a miraculous creation of form, structure and *musical* content.

No composer of the past hundred years has evoked more controversy than Stravinsky. From the time when he provoked a Parisian audience (for once caught off balance by an unfamiliar idiom) to acts of violence and insult, the academic world has been arraigned against him. And not a few ardent followers who rightly discerned his power as manifest by the earlier works, have failed to keep step with this man who never seems to repeat himself. Books and articles are today bristling with statements that the later music of Stravinsky is arid, empty or baffling.

Stravinsky has moved steadily towards a more universal musical language. If he once employed powerful tone color and juxtaposition to achieve certain ends, and then later in his progression he elects to make use of quite opposite means, his approach to the problem still retains its unique vitality and its musical logic. What he has accomplished has a certain parallel with the experiences of a documentary film director. This director once filmed the exotic shapes and colors of the jungle, and thereby made a great reputation. His next film, equally perceptive, was of the subtleties of the desert. Both the jungle and the desert had been seen and recorded by the same sensitive man employing the same camera, but the audience which apparently understood one, could not grasp the other. The Stravinsky who created LE SACRE is the same musical mind as that which produced ORPHEUS — an antithesis which is a hallmark of his genius.

This is not an attempted analysis or an explanation of Stravinsky's creative processes. But if much music of the

Romanticists can be described as an all too human literature in which great or petty emotions are furnished with musical equivalents, Stravinsky stands in bold relief as a creator of musical ideas which have an existence and form wholly independent of allegory or program.

In his Harvard lectures, *The Poetics of Music,* Stravinsky has written clearly on the subject of his work. It is possibly unfair to quote random sentences from such a closely reasoned essay, but some of his statements are particularly pertinent to this article. He says, for instance: "The study of the creative process is an extremely delicate one. It is impossible to observe the inner workings of this process from the outside. It is futile to follow its successive phases in someone else's work. It is likewise very difficult to observe one's self." Later in the same chapter he states: "This appetite that is aroused in me at the mere thought of putting in order musical elements that have attracted my attention is not at all a fortuitous thing like inspiration, but as habitual and periodic, if not as constant, as a natural need." Another very illuminating sentence is: "Thus, what concerns us here is not imagination in itself, but rather creative imagination: the faculty that helps us to pass from the level of conception to the level of realization." One more quote is included from these Harvard lectures (published by the Harvard University Press) because of its application to this subject: "I do not have a temperament suitable to academicism; so I always use academic formulas knowingly and voluntarily.

I use them quite as knowingly as I would use folklore. They are raw materials of my work."

Take the case of contemporary sounds in this mechanized world. Elements which many composers have introduced into their music with unwarranted gestures appear in certain works of Stravinsky naturally and with complete fulfillment of intention. Antheil's *Ballet Méchanique,* Mossolov's *Iron Foundry* and Honneger's *Pacific 231* are typical examples of "lifting" almost unchanged the cacophony of the machine. This has been unsuccessful to the same degree as Fernand Leger's paintings based directly on the anatomy of machinery. Picasso has employed certain machine-like forms — but uses them as *digested* or assimilated elements in contemporary painting. Stravinsky's understanding of machinery and jazz has manifested itself similarly. These elements are used as natural properties he has elected to emphasize. Russian folk songs are recognized in certain earlier Stravinsky works, but they have been energized or "stepped up" by him. His very individual caldron has metamorphosed them, for the legitimate uses of musical form, often with results not unlike our jazz. Yet the works of Stravinsky which may be reminiscent of machinery or jazz have really nothing to do, directly, with either. They are simply the materials of our time used as components in the total scheme for building a musical structure.

It is difficult to recall any creative artist in any field who has explored more possibilities and broadened more horizons, yet Stravinsky has always remained within the framework of

European music. By comparison, a Debussy, influenced by the music of the Orient, and Schoenberg, with his preoccupation with the twelve-tone scale, are outlaws; while Varèse, on the other hand, is a true revolutionary. Stravinsky brutally upset classical traditions only for the purpose of reutilizing them. He grasped the strands extending from a very traditional tapestry, and proceeded to weave patterns never before seen on the loom. But he employed the same strands, and the same loom! The strangeness may be the result of its double distillation; he has made pure music aware of itself for the first time since the vigorous orderliness of Bach.

The music of Stravinsky needs to be heard. As T. S. Eliot has said: "The multiplication of critical books and essays may create, and I have seen it create, a vicious taste for reading about works of art instead of reading the works themselves, it may supply opinion instead of educating taste."

After all the essays about the music of Stravinsky, plus all the analytical studies, have been read, there remains an enigma about Stravinsky that will never be found by the critical surgeons who minutely examine every measure of his astounding list of musical inventions. For a music which has remained within the Occidental culture it is disturbingly exciting in the best primitive sense. As a composer, there is an exclusion of self and an impersonality about much of his work; and yet, ambiguously enough, one can always identify it at once as Stravinsky. It could be none other.

Stravinsky's critics have found most of his inventions since

LES NOCES sterile or cerebral. But to see Stravinsky in true perspective, we must see him whole. You cannot honestly divide him into little sections, and submit each to the microscope, and come up with a true measure of his stature. What will these dissenters do about HISTORY OF THE SOLDIER, APOLLON MUSAGETÉS, CONCERTO FOR TWO PIANOS, or the new MASS, his first large liturgical work, not to mention SYMPHONY OF PSALMS. The MASS is impersonal in the manner of the pre-Bach composers, and a truly Gothic edifice. And even when we examine any one of these works separately, and subject them to any standard of criticism, the conclusion must be governed by one dominant characteristic: it is the work of a musical mind so selective, inventive and prolific as to be indubitably one of music's greatest men. Here is a composer who draws his strength from sources as fundamental as those tapped by the scientist and the engineer.

S A M U E L   D U S H K I N

1949   Working with Stravinsky

I.

One evening in Paris in 1930 my publisher and friend, Willy Strecker, the head of the music publishing house of Schott & Sons, and I were discussing contemporary music in general and contemporary violin music in particular. Both of us felt that if Stravinsky could be induced to compose a concerto for violin and orchestra, a very important contribution to violin music would be achieved. We decided to approach Stravinsky with our suggestion. As I had never met Stravinsky, Strecker, who knew him, agreed to talk to him.

A few weeks later while I was playing in Germany, I received a telegram from Strecker asking me to come to his home in Wiesbaden as soon as possible because Stravinsky, who was conducting in Wiesbaden at the moment, was interested in writing a concerto for violin and orchestra. He added that Stravinsky wanted me to be near him during the time that he was composing the concerto. I was pleased at Stravinsky's attitude because I remembered that many of the great violin concertos were written with the advice of a contemporary violinist. The Brahms violin concerto was composed in close collaboration with Joachim, and even Mendelssohn, who himself played the violin, asked his friend Ferdinand David to help him, as David was more experienced as a violinist-performer.

On my way to Wiesbaden I was rather nervous. I had always heard that Stravinsky was difficult and could be curt if he did not like someone. I remembered the story of the pianist in Paris, who went up to Stravinsky during the intermission at a concert and said, *"Maître,* when may I come to see you?" Stravinsky took out his little engagement book, started turning the leaves, saying, *"Pas lundi, pas mardi, pas mercredi,"* ("not Monday, not Tuesday, not Wednesday"), then stopped, looked up and said, *"Jamais, Monsieur!"* ("NEVER, Monsieur!")

180

Our first meeting could not have taken place in a warmer, more friendly atmosphere than the Strecker home in Wiesbaden. Here, among friends, his personal charm was evident at once. It was not long before I realized that he was not only capable of giving tenderness and affection but seemed to be in great need of them himself. In fact, I sensed very soon something tense and auguished about him which made one want to comfort and reassure *him*. The Stravinsky I had heard about and imagined and the Igor Fiodorovitch I met seemed two different people. I think little five-year-old Olga Strecker expressed my first impressions perfectly. Stravinsky adores children and played with the Strecker children constantly when he was there. They called him "Igor." One day little Olga, after having overheard days of heated discussion among her elders about Stravinsky, asked her mother, *"Wer ist der Stravinsky?"* ("Who is that Stravinsky?") Mrs. Strecker said, "Why, you know, that's 'Igor,' the one you love to play with all the time." Little Olga exclaimed, *"Wie soll ich wissen das der Stravinsky der Igor ist?"* ("How should I know that that Stravinsky is that Igor?")

The evening at the Strecker's was a great success, and the following day we came to a perfect understanding. As soon as Stravinsky could begin to work, I was to join him in Nice, where he then lived. At that time he travelled during the winter, playing and conducting, and composed from early spring until late fall.

During the winter I saw Stravinsky in Paris quite often. One day when we were lunching in a restaurant, Stravinsky took out a piece of paper and wrote down this chord and asked me if it could be played. I had never seen a chord with such an enormous stretch, from the "E" to the top "A," and I said, "No." Stravinsky said sadly, *"Quel dommage."* ("What a pity.") After I got home, I tried it, and, to my astonishment, I found that in that register, the stretch of the eleventh was relatively easy to play, and the  sound fascinated me. I telephoned Stravinsky at once to tell him that it could be done. When the concerto was finished, more than six months later, I understood his disappointment when I first said, "No." This chord, in a different dress, begins each of the four movements. Stravinsky himself calls it his "passport" to that concerto.

II.

The Stravinsky family lived in a house just outside Nice on the way to Monte Carlo. The family consisted of his elderly mother, his wife and their two sons and two daughters. Stravinsky's mother was a strong-minded character who though she was proud of her son and adored him never submitted to his equally strong will. She had been brought up on the music which Stravinsky's father, a famous bass,

182

had sung in Russia, so that her son's music continually posed problems for her. I remember a few years later in Paris on the twenty-fifth anniversary of the performance of Stravinsky's "Rites of Spring," which his mother had never heard except on records, my wife, before the performance, asked Mme. Stravinsky, "Aren't you thrilled to hear the 'Sacre' at last in a concert hall?" *"Je pense que ça ne sera pas de la musique pour moi,"* ("I think that it will not be music for me,") she answered. *"J'espére que vous ne sifflerez pas,"* ("I hope you will not whistle"), my wife said. *"Non, parce que je ne sais pas siffler,"* ("No, because I do not know how to whistle"), she replied.

Stravinsky's wife was a highly-cultured and aesthetic person, who devoted her life to her home and children.

Stravinsky's study was on the top floor of the house. What struck me at once was the extraordinary neatness and order of this study. On his desk, within easy reach, were all sorts of gadgets. I was particularly struck by the fact that he did not use music paper for his first sketches. He uses a book with plain white pages. On these blank sheets he draws the five staff lines according to his needs of the moment with a diminutive roller made specially for him. Some staves are longer, some shorter, sometimes just one line, sometimes several lines, so that when the page is finished, it looks like a strangely designed drawing, and each page looks different from the preceding page.

When he is working, Stravinsky is always in a hyper-sensitive state. Everything that occurs seems to be magnified. At first I was astonished at how slowly he worked. He often composes at the piano, intensely concentrated, grunting and struggling to find the notes and chords he seems to be hearing. It was amazing to realize that so complex a score as the "Sacre du Printemps" was composed like this.

During the intervals between work when we had tea together every afternoon in his study, Stravinsky would talk about general and personal experiences. These conversations from the very beginning meant a great deal to me. One day when I came to work with him from Antibes where I was staying, I found him very agitated. "I haven't had my sleep," he explained. "I was awakened at dawn this morning by a little bird singing on my window sill. For the first five minutes I was fascinated. But the bird went on singing!" After *ten* minutes, I wanted to kill that bird. But the bird went on singing. And, do you know, after fifteen minutes, I was again fascinated." Another day I found him rather worried about himself, and I asked him what was the matter. He said, "Oh my intestines, my intestines!" "Do they hurt?" I asked. "No, they don't hurt," he answered, "but they keep saying, 'We are here, we are here.'"

When the work was going painfully slowly, Stravinsky, who is a very religious man, would talk to me about faith. "You must have faith," he would say. "When I was younger,

À Igor Strawinsky
en souvenir de l'Oiseau
Marc Chagall 1949. de Feu. Paris

Russell
Cowles

4

and ideas didn't come, I felt desperate and thought everything was finished. But now I have faith, and I know ideas will come. The waiting in anguish is the price one must pay." Once when we were walking in his garden, Stravinsky said, "First ideas are very important; they come from God. And if after working and working and working, I return to these ideas, then I know they're good."

Stravinsky's illustration of rhythm has been of great help to me ever since in appreciating rhythm in all music. I had noticed that a certain rhythmic accompaniment he had written was at first somewhat symmetrical. After he had altered and altered it, the number of pulsations remained the same, but the symmetry was completely gone and the personality of the rhythmic pattern was new. I asked him if he could define rhythm, and he said that he could perhaps explain what he felt by comparing rhythm with mathematics. "In mathematics," he said, "there are an infinite number of ways of arriving at the number seven. It's the same with rhythm. The difference is that whereas in mathematics the *sum* is the important thing; it makes no difference if you say five and two, or two and five, six and one or one and six, and so on. With rhythm, however, the fact that they add up to seven is of secondary importance. The important thing is, is it five and two or is it two and five, because five and two is a different person from two and five."

III.

My function was to advise Stravinsky how his ideas could best be adapted to the exigencies of the violin as a concert display instrument. At various intervals he would show me what he had just written, sometimes a page, sometimes only a few lines, sometimes half a movement. Then we discussed whatever suggestions I was able to make. Whenever he accepted one of my suggestions, even a simple change such as extending the range of the violin by stretching the phrase to the octave below and the octave above, Stravinsky would insist on altering the very foundations correspondingly. He behaved like an architect who if asked to change a room on the third floor had to go down to the foundations to keep the proportions of his whole structure.

There were times when I would arrange a passage for the violin and play it to him and he would say, "Yes, that's fine, but it's from another opera." Once when I was particularly pleased with the way I had arranged a brilliant violinistic passage and tried to insist on his keeping it, he said: "You remind me of a salesman at the *Galeries Lafayette*. You say, 'Isn't this brilliant, isn't this exquisite, look at the beautiful colors, everybody's wearing it.' I say, 'Yes, it is brilliant, it is beautiful, everyone is wearing it — I don't want it.'"

Stravinsky's music is so original and so personal that it constantly posed new problems of technique and sound for the violin. These problems often touched the very core of the composition itself and led to most of our discussions.

A mutual friend of ours once asked Stravinsky, "How do you find Sam to work with?" He answered: "When I show Sam a new passage, he is deeply moved, very excited — then a few days later he asks me to make changes."

After watching Stravinsky work and rework and make changes, I often thought of Paul Valery's aphorism: *"Un artiste se juge par la qualité de ses refus."* ("An artist is judged by the quality of what he discards.")

Once I thought I would surprise him by making an arrangement of the *berceuse* from "The Fire Bird." After I had played it for him, he looked unhappy. I felt slightly hurt. "Don't you like it?" I asked. "It sounds like Kreisler's arrangement of Rimsky-Korsakoff's 'Chant Hindou,'" he said. "Well," I said, "it *is* rather Oriental, isn't it?" Stravinsky lowered his head and said sadly, "Yes, I'm afraid that's the trouble with it."

I abandoned the idea of transcriptions for the time being, but, fortunately, after the violin concerto and the "Duo Concertant" were composed, we made a great many transcriptions together for our violin and piano programs for our concert tours. Curiously enough, one of the transcriptions we made was of the *berceuse* from "The Fire Bird." All of our other transcriptions were difficult to perform, so I thought I would be very practical and suggested that the *berceuse* would lend itself to an easy arrangement which anyone could play. But we had not gone very far before Stravinsky became so interested in rewriting it that it was becoming very difficult again. I remarked that not many would be able to play the new version. Stravinsky, now concentrated on his work, got angry and said, *"Qu'est ce que cela peut me faire si tous les imbeciles ne jouent pas ma musique."* ("What can it matter to me if all the fools do not play my music.")

There are two ways of approaching the problem of arrangements. One is to make playable music for the desired instrument. The other is to go back to the essence of the music and rewrite or recreate the music in the spirit of the new instrument. Stravinsky was interested only in the latter. I was happy that he felt that way as that had always been my own aim in making transcriptions.

IV.

Before the end of the summer of 1931 when Stravinsky was just beginning the last movement of the concerto, he and his family moved to Voreppe, a small village near Grenoble. As the first performance was to take place in Berlin in October with the Berliner Rundfunk Orchestra, I was beginning to get worried about learning it in time. The last movement, however, progressed very smoothly, and I was able to study the first three movements while he was finishing the last.

The first performance took place in Berlin at the Philharmonie to a capacity audience. It was a great success. Discussions were plentiful during the days following the performance as always after a new Stravinsky work. The press was divided, as usual. Some critics were very enthusiastic. Some criticisms were vicious, as usual. Stravinsky was very angry. "Why are you so upset?" I asked him. "Hasn't it always been so? Even Voltaire so long ago said of critics, *'Le critique est pour l'artiste ce qu'est une mouche sur un cheval de course. Elle le pique mais elle ne l'arréte pas.'*" ("The critic is to the artist what a fly is on a race horse. It stings him but doesn't stop him.") He liked that, but as it did not quite calm him, I said, "No one can please everyone." Knowing him to be religious, I risked adding, "Even God doesn't please everyone." He jumped up and shouted, *"Especially* God!"

That winter, after the premiere in Berlin, we played the concerto in other cities in Germany, and then in London, Paris, Florence, Madrid, in Switzerland, Belgium, Holland and the Scandinavian countries. Later we played it in the United States. It was after our long European tour that Stravinsky decided to write a duo for violin and piano, a work in which each instrument would be of equal importance. This composition became the now well-known "Duo Concertant." His idea was to have a violin and piano program which could be played in more places than concerts with orchestra, because

189

concerts with orchestra require so many rehearsals before each performance.

We planned to make new arrangements of his "Suite ıtalienne" on Pergolesi themes and the "Divertimento" on Tschaikowsky themes. These with the new work, the "Duo Concertant," would give us the major part of a recital program. We also felt the need for a group of shorter pieces to complete our program, which would then represent various phases of Stravinsky's musical creation.

I was delighted with Stravinsky's idea, not only because it enabled me to collaborate further with him, but it promised a great enrichment of the literature for the violin, which has always been poor in shorter pieces of quality.

My role was to extract from the original scores of former works we were transcribing, a violin part which I thought appropriate for the violin as a virtuoso instrument and characteristic of his musical intentions. After I had written out the violin part, we would meet, and Stravinsky then wrote the piano part which very often resulted in something different from the original composition. Stravinsky sometimes also altered details of the violin parts which I had extracted. I believe I am not exaggerating when I say that Stravinsky has thus given us a series of short pieces for violin and piano which, although they are transcriptions, have the flavor and authenticity of original works.

V.

Working, travelling and living with Stravinsky, as I did for about six years, was always stimulating, sometimes difficult, but never banal or boring. His energy and vitality are astounding, and he has a power of concentration greater than that of any other person I have ever known. Even in his relaxation there seems to be a concentrated will power.

While on a concert tour one is asked a lot of questions. I have always been delighted with Stravinsky's sharp and witty answers. Once someone asked him, "Why is there such a difference between the 'Sacre' and the 'Psaumes'? Can you tell me what *is* the difference?" "Yes," said Stravinsky. "The difference is twenty years." Another time a very attractive young lady, whom Stravinsky evidently thought charming, and amiably and patiently answered many of her questions, felt encouraged to make a confession. She said, "I feel so much when I hear 'Firebird' and 'Petroushka.' Why can't I feel anything in your later works?" "My dear, for that you'll have to consult your doctor," Stravinsky replied.

I noticed that when people never mentioned any of his other works, but swooned over "Firebird" and "Petroushka," he always resented it. I learned later that a well known musician had come to him to commission a concerto, but the project fell through because he wanted music like "Petroushka" or "Firebird." In Hollywood, where Stravinsky now lives, he

191

has always been asked to write something like "Petroushka" for the movies. One day Stravinsky said to me: "You see, my tragedy is that the world likes 'Petroushka.'" Jokingly, I said: "Well, if you want to get rich, why don't you write something like that again?" "It would cost *me* more," he answered.

I was startled when one of my musical friends said to me: "Of course, I admire and respect Stravinsky, and I take off my hat to him, but I must confess I cannot understand his music. It's not my language." I repeated this to Stravinsky, wondering what he would say. "Of course, it's not *his* language," Stravinsky said, "it's *mine!*"

One of the many things that I am grateful to Stravinsky for is that in working with him I had to make a real effort to learn *his* language. That experience taught me that the same kind of effort is necessary to assimilate other trends in contemporary music.

After all, Stravinsky's music exists; it is here; it is we who will not be here for long.

13

L A W R E N C E   M O R T O N

1949   Incongruity and Faith

I do not know if it happens in every work, but it occurs frequently enough to be counted now as one of the characteristic attitudes that inform the music of Stravinsky.

I am talking about his cultivation of incongruity. Rather than define it I shall cite as an example the quotation of Schubert's MARCHE MILITAIRE in the CIRCUS POLKA. Operating here is a whole complex of incongruities: Stravinsky, who dedicated his SYMPHONY OF PSALMS to the glory of God, writes music for a circus which is dedicated to the pleasure of man.

It is played not by one of the world's great orchestras under a Monteux or an Ansermet, but by a band whose leader is, I would presume, more at home among the pretty banalities of THE SKATER'S WALTZ. Elephants, the clumsiest of nature's creatures, are taught to imitate what is properly the business of the most graceful. The musical intelligentsia, for whom every new work of Stravinsky is a major artistic event, go a-slumming to Madison Square Garden in order to listen to what they would normally hear in Carnegie Hall. There is a dreamlike quality about the whole business. Values seem to be turned upside down. Elephants become critics: they don't like the music, we are told; it has no rhythm. This is not insanity; it is all for fun. In the circumstances it is not surprising that Stravinsky quotes Schubert. Indeed, it would have been shocking if he had *not*. For how else could he have crowned the whole fantasy with a whopper that even the basest groundling could understand?

I cite other examples: Stravinsky employs popular dance forms (tango, waltz, ragtime) in L'HISTOIRE DU SOLDAT, a drama that is concerned with an ethical problem of the most profound and universal seriousness, the problem of good and evil; and he uses the chorale, a form associated with sacred music, to accompany an embrace. In SCÈNES DE BALLET, a work written for, of all people, Billy Rose, there is a trumpet tune of almost incredible sentimentality. I know nothing quite like it anywhere else in Stravinsky's music. Remove from it the marks of genius, make it four-square, give it a Cole Porter lyric, and you have a genuine pop-tune. As it stands, however, it is a solemnization of Broadway, a halo for a chorus girl, a portrait of Mr. Rose as Diaghilev. Why should it be? Merely because *The Seven Lively Arts,* for which it was written, was a pretentious production, rich in snob values. This could not be said; but it could be sung, especially by Broadway's most expressive instrument, the trumpet. No critic could have written a sharper commentary on the show than did Stravinsky. But it was a gentle ribbing, the storm was tempered to the shorn lamb, for the composer is as humane as he is discerning.

This is the method of incongruity. It brings into juxtaposition ideas that are normally widely separated. It yokes the ox with the unicorn, to draw a gilded carriage in which a washerwoman rides. It lets the princess marry a swineherd who is not a prince in disguise, and it casts Bob Hope as Prospero. It is most common as a literary device. It served Dean Swift well in *Gulliver's Travels* and it allowed Defoe to put the loftiest sentiments into the mouths of his lusty heroines. It makes Hamlet's answers to Polonius apparent nonsense that is actually full of meaning. But perhaps the classic example of the method is Alexander Pope's *The Rape of the Lock,* where the whole machinery of epic poetry is put to work to expound an absurdity:

> "What dire offence from am'rous causes springs,
> What mighty contests rise from trivial things,
> I sing."

And the poet sings through five cantos and some eight hundred lines of verse about a minor social scandal. The whole of the matter is in the manner, and the manner itself is a compendium of the ideas and sentiments that made Pope's contemporaries behave as they did. At the center of Pope's style is the epigram, with the rhymed couplet and the mid-line pause. And one hears something like this in the DANSES CONCERTANTES, where the movement is constantly interrupted by cadences, and where incipient lyricism is cut at the bud.

Stravinsky did not invent this methodology in music. As one would expect, there are antecedents in earlier music, in the quodlibets that provided entertainment at the gatherings of the Bach clan, in Mozart's *Musical Joke* with its gentle jibes at clumsy players and still clumsier composers. Most delightful of all is Haydn's SYMPHONY NO. 80 in D-Minor (one of Alfred Einstein's recent restorations) which plunges in its first movement into a very serious discussion of Large Issues, for which it laughingly apologizes before the exposition is over by an almost ridiculous little waltz-tune coda. One does not philosophize thus in polite society, Haydn seems to be saying. And having proferred his excuses, he tops the joke in the development section by making a Large Issue out of the waltz tune. And there is Beethoven's example in the gigantic set of variations he wrote on Diabelli's trivial theme.

If incongruity is a methodology in art, it is also an attitude toward life, and that is why it is important. A commentator

196

on one of Stravinsky's works borrowed from Emerson the image of the artist taking a look at things from between his legs. It is a deflationary technique, and a remarkably apt one when contemplating the grandiosities of the nineteenth century. It exposes the excesses of an esthetic that began legitimately enough with the notion that self-expression was one of the things that music could decently traffic in, but ended with the unfortunate discovery that hysteria and self-flagellation paid greater dividends. This was something more than the decadence of Romanticism. It was indeed a symptom of world sickness. The love-and-death psychoses of Wagner and his followers, the deep abiding pessimism of Mahler, the gaudy trappings beneath which Strauss attempted to hide his vulgarity, the sensual mysticism of Scriabin, all of these were evidences of a social decay that perforce culminated in catastrophe, in World War I.

The reaction too was inevitable. The search for values necessarily led in the opposite direction, toward sanity, toward (in Stravinsky's terms) order and discipline, toward the Apollonian esthetic. Unfortunately the direction came to be known as "back," although it could better have been designated "across." And when the term "neo-classicism" came into prominence it quickly earned the implication of "pseudo-classicism," which was fastened to it by its opponents. (The term "atonality" has similarly been of disservice to the Schoenberg school.) The resulting war of words sometimes obscured the real issues. But they are clear enough today. If we cannot always say in words

197

precisely what today's classicism *is,* we can at least say what it is *not.* For plainly it denies. It denies not necessarily the nineteenth century itself, *in toto,* but certainly the decline of that century's esthetic into sheer bathos, its shift from self-expression to self-pity. If we cannot define our classicism we can at least exhibit it, on that high but unspeakable level where it is exemplified by Stravinsky's work.

In that work the element of denial is strong, though not so strong as in the speech and writing. Consider Stravinsky's attitude toward Tchaikowsky. To those who think of Tchaikowsky in terms of the morbid and tempestuous composer of the PATHÉTIQUE, it must have come as something of a shock when Stravinsky apotheosized his work in BAISER DE LA FÉE. There was no reference to tears and temper. In Stravinsky's view there is a basic incongruity (not to say injustice) in the way the world has come to prefer the symphonic to the ballet music. This he has pointed up by reviewing the spirit of the dance music in all its charm and fastidiousness, with the implication that it is perhaps time to revalue our valuation of Tchaikowsky even if it means a denial of the pleasures of melancholy. It is this same preference for urbanity that has made Stravinsky single out for praise, among all the purveyors of Romantic emotion, Chabrier, Delibes, Weber, Gounod and the early Verdi. These were not, to be sure, the great men of the century; but neither were they the men who propelled the century toward the abyss into which it finally fell. There is danger here, of course; the danger of valuing manner above matter, style above content, the shape of things above their spirit. It is the danger of formalism, to which the spirit of classicism has surrendered before. But it does not threaten Stravinsky the composer, although it sometimes threatens Stravinsky the teacher and apologist. This means only that he is not quite the artist with words that he is with sounds. And it is just as well that this is so; for were it otherwise we might have lost a great composer and gained thereby merely another critic.

Let no one think that because his denials are strong his affirmations are weak. Modesty is not one of his vices, and his punctuation system does not exclude the exclamation point delivered by horns and trombones. Let us observe that one can say "I affirm!" without giving it the inflection of "I accuse!"

And now to my conclusions. For the most part the technique of incongruity manifests itself as parody or caricature. The music is full of paradoxes, epigrams, figures of speech. They are often, I suggest, the very subject matter of the music. And therefore one might say that Stravinsky composes music about his intellectual experiences just as last century's composers wrote music about their emotional experiences. I have no wish to set up for further fruitless argument the old dichotomy of intellect and emotion. Psychology has given us some practical information about these matters, although artists and estheticians prefer to ignore it lest they run out of material for their beloved controversies. We concede that Wagner, who has become the arch enemy of our generation, was yet an artist of consummate intellectual prowess, and that the facture of his music is beyond reproach. We admit, too, that Mozart with his G-MINOR SYMPHONY could reach far beyond his time and into the troubled areas of the next century. And we see too that Stravinsky can make the large Beethovenish gesture, as he does in the opening of the SYMPHONY IN THREE MOVEMENTS. That emotion and intellect are not mutually exclusive is a commonplace that should not require recapitulation. But that the adventures of the mind, no less than the adventures of the heart, can be the subject of musical discourse, is a commonplace that still needs shouting from the housetops. The order and discipline with which this music is formulated are in fact an expression of faith that our generation much needs. And the emotion generated by them is indeed complete enough, absorbing and satisfying enough, to lift the spirit far beyond the time we spend in actually listening to music. Could the statesmen of the world order and discipline the world's affairs half as efficiently and beautifully as Stravinsky arranges the notes of an E-minor triad, then indeed the millennium would be on its way. There is, in other words, a moral strength, an ethical purpose, in Stravinsky's esthetic ideals. This is not to say that his artistic faith is the only possible one for this epoch. But it is one that has proved itself in works, has inspired the creativity of our generation of artists, and corresponds to the facts of our lives.

Indeed, has it not given our age its very name, The Age of Stravinsky?

14

R O B E R T   C R A F T

1949 Stravinsky's Mass: A Notebook

In a conversation with Evelyn Waugh, Stravinsky said: "My MASS was not composed for concert performances but for use in the church. It is liturgical and almost without ornament. In making a musical setting of the Credo I wished only to preserve the text in a special way. One composes a march to facilitate marching men, so with my Credo I hope to provide an aid to the text. The Credo is the longest movement. There is much to believe." Later — "Liturgical music has practically disappeared, except, of course, the third rate academic kind.

201

The tradition has been lost. Look at the Victorian hymnology which compressed into four-squares and brutally harmonized the most beautiful plainsongs. In Los Angeles one hears anything in church, Rachmaninoff, Tristan and Isolde. The Credo is a kind of contact with God."

* * * * *

From the view of a century the Church would offer no consistent tradition. Periodic interdictions against contrapuntal music — as Cranmer's attack on the *Masses* of Byrd — resulted in the alternation of opposed styles. The view of a thousand years reveals a composite heritage, however, pejorative. One can only trace phases in the breakdown of culture as, properly, the awareness of secular and its isolation and, later, the awareness of sacred and its separation. Monsignor Ronald Knox, "The Mass is really a kind of religious dance."

* * * * *

One often ignores the merely practical question of the accessibility of music. Stravinsky has a deep admiration for the 14th century madrigals of Jacopo da Bologna. What 18th or 19th century composer could have even known the music? Indeed, no 18th or 19th century composer could have heard, much less have the habit of the great bulk of Renaissance music.

* * * * *

M. Ansermet called Stravinsky's MASS a work of "humility and submission." If you do not believe man is a fallen creature, you cannot recognize the qualities. But, is the MASS more humble than the SYMPHONY IN C or OEDIPUS? I think not, and that therefore Stravinsky is to be judged as a whole. Who is surprised with the MASS or with Stravinsky for composing a Mass has escaped his significance.

The problem of assimilation. The MASS evidences several models, all exquisitely interfused. Ultimately every bar is only and unmistakably Stravinsky. The Credo is redolent of plain-song, has a canonic Amen and a Plagal cadence. There is an exquisite use of Organum in the Gloria and an amazing revival of Gregorian Neumes in the Sanctus. The latter, for instance, contains a Climacus Resupinus Flexus, in modern notational cognates, of course.

The concertante-ripieno vocal style reconstitutes the oldest Psalmic Graduale-Response idea of the liturgy. It is also a very principle of Stravinsky in each work. In the Gloria two solo voices forte alternate with the chorus piano. In the Sanctus the fugue for solo voices is answered by a real tutti Hosanna. The Agnus Dei contrasts instruments and chorus. The orchestra's four 4-bar phrases do not touch the 3 chorus phrases they interrupt.

* * * * *

A major and infrequently mentioned shift effected by Stravinsky is his emphasis on the Phrygian. The profusion of examples from earlier works, the 6th chord which ends MAVRA, the first movement of PSAUMES, seem to prophecy the haunting and Phrygian ORPHEUS. An interesting comparison thrusts itself between the two-voice fugue which ends ORPHEUS (Sept. 1947) and the fugue of the Sanctus (Jan. 1948). Both are Phrygian, both employ a new rhythmic idea: a short accented note on the beat quickly slurring to a long note whose syncopation is absorbed by its length.

The MASS is also marked by the use of the Dorian mode. In the Kyrie the word Christie is treated fugually by the chorus over a figure for oboes and bassoons that might have been an accompaniment by Henry Purcell. The Dorian is ended by an extraordinary modulation to D in which the chorus stops at the leading tone and the D is left to the three quiet instruments.

The MASS ends Dorian in an apotheosis which is a kind of musical palindrome. The lines of the top oboe and of the two bassoons are exactly the same backwards or forwards. The effect of these last two woodwind bars, Dorian after the quiet brass with its mixed C and C sharp, is serene and complete.

*　　*　　*　　*　　*

The MASS is another Stravinsky work which does not fall into the concert categories. The horned imperatives of symphonic program, solo recital program, chamber music and choral concert, opera, have all but wiped out some of the major literatures of music. Because we have no medium for the performance of Bach's Cantatas, we do not have the habit of them and therefore fail to see that the organ and chamber music is not John Sebastian Bach's greatest. Most Monteverdi is lost to us, as well as a thousand others; now those 18th century symphonies are destroyed on "symphonic" programs. Stravinsky composes another work which demands not only a familiarity with obsolescent cultures but a new or revived performance hierarchy. Isn't this the problem with NOCES, HISTOIRE, RENARD, MAVRA?

Stravinsky's MASS is Roman Catholic. He is by birth and education Greek Orthodox. Learned in the dogmas and forms of both, he is immensely concerned with the "place" of art in, say, St. Basil and St. Thomas. Stravinsky is predominantly Roman Catholic but always with that rare angle from 6th century Ravenna. Since NOCES (1914-17) the fiercely sacred Byzantine without Purgatory and the third dimension has been supplanted, and in March of 1949 he arranged his Russian Pater Noster and Ave Maria for the Roman Catholic Church, an arrangement which brings them closer to the Credo of the MASS.

The MASS itself is completely Roman Catholic. In a contrapuntal work this can only mean that it has avoided John Sebastian Bach. Certainly no single model was uppermost, and none at all of the last three centuries.

*　　*　　*　　*　　*

The Kyries has sections, blocks of tonalities. In only 52 bars there are cadences in seven keys. It concludes on a G 6th, which is approached, one might say, justified, from four different cadence tones simultaneously. If the movement opened in C minor, a progression of keys might be charted with complacency, but the stark cries of E flats and C's which are sounded at the beginning only prepare the chorus for an equi-librated A flat, which is recapitulated exactly and which might be a kind of harmonic appogiatura to the final G. One could write a book on the systems of keys in this little piece, and be positively rapturous at how ingeniously the C sharp of A becomes the pivot for D flat.

*　*　*　*　*

The orchestra which Stravinsky says "tunes" his choir never plays quite the same music. It adds tones, sounds different root tones than appear in the vocal parts, stresses, underlines, imitates, counterpoints, sets off and augments the chorus. The proportions of two oboes, English horn, two bassoons, two trumpets and three trombones demand a small choir, prefer-ably with boy treble timbre. The sonority is altogether unlike anything before, including Stravinsky. The instrumentation is remarkable in the way it supports without doubling, often while weaving lines distinct from the chorus as the trombone fragments in the Credo. "Only God can create. I make music from music."

*　*　*　*　*

Stravinsky introduced his MASS today. How was it heard? Discount the hypothesis of normality, but were each to try with Ramuz, *"Continuer à etre etonne; continuer à etre neuf et jusq'au bout devant ce qui est neuf; car tout est neuf pour qui est neuf."*

206

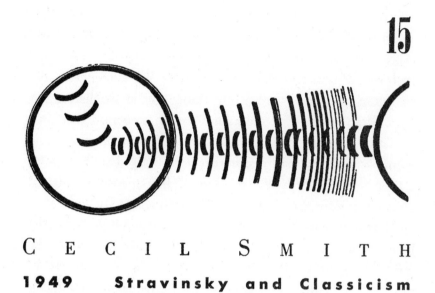

15

C E C I L S M I T H

1949   Stravinsky and Classicism

In the United States, no composer's aims have been more stubbornly misunderstood by his antagonists than those of Igor Stravinsky. Those who consider his music heartless and lacking in juice are fond of quoting his views on musical aesthetics and theory quite out of context, in the hope of discrediting both the opinions and the compositions that exemplify them. Without wishing to champion Stravinsky's position and accomplishments at the expense of other contemporary composers whose music, in varying degrees, I also admire and respect, I should nevertheless like in these paragraphs to try to render him his due as a vital and constructive influence upon American musical thinking and experience.

Even Arnold Schönberg, though he has by no means had an easy time of it, has not suffered as large an amount and degree of caricature and undervaluation, from laymen and professional musicians alike, as Stravinsky. No matter what discomfiture they may create in those who hear his music, Schönberg's twelve-tone procedures are so categorical that their intellectual nature is quite clear; and his compositions, being highly subjective, may appropriately be judged and disposed of, for better or for worse, in terms of the amount of personal pleasure or pain they induce in each individual listener.

Stravinsky arouses antipathy in many of his hearers because he does not concede that this is a proper criterion. Those who say, "I like THE FIREBIRD, but I cannot get any pleasure out of the arid pieces he writes nowadays," are demanding of music an overt appeal to the emotions which Stravinsky long since refused to try to make. The fact that he steadfastly refrains from seeking to win back THE FIREBIRD type of audience by any of his new works constitutes a tribute to the firm reality of his convictions, since THE FIREBIRD (or perhaps PETROUCHKA, which offers similar bids for an emotionalized popular response) is certainly the most profitable source of revenue in the entire catalog of his works.

But ever since LES NOCES and L'HISTOIRE DU SOLDAT, Stravinsky has been the arch-enemy of decadent Romanticism, whose aim is to impress, stun, stimulate, cajole, lull, charm, and seduce the audience. By casting aspersions upon the "expressive" qualities of Romantic music — by denying that a big wash of emotional-ism is a more central value in music than clarity and integrity of construction — Stravinsky, more than any other single com-poser, has made our generation stop and think what music ought to be like in the mid-twentieth century. But since think-ing is less comfortable than repeating past formulas, both those who would like to compose music without posing new problems for themselves and those who prefer to listen to music as a form of self-indulgence are deeply annoyed by Stravinsky's challenge to their complacency.

Before the last war, the most determined opposition to Stravinsky came from those whose musical metabolism required a luscious diet of Strauss, Sibelius, and Rachmaninoff. This group is now diminishing in size, if the present abrupt and agreeable disappearance of Sibelius and shrinkage of Strauss in our orchestra programs may be taken as an index. (Rach-maninoff will survive, of course, as long as pianists dream of riding to success on the plush-cushioned orchestration of the C Minor Concerto.)

But a new postwar phalanx is arising to reinforce the old one. In Europe, Stravinsky has begun to be shown the way to the door. The neo-Romanticism of Luigi Dallapiccola, Olivier Messiaen, Vladimir Vogel, and various others who share their predilection is the current diet of most of the new-music coteries. In some instances, as in the post-Franckian mysticism of Messiaen, this music is essentially a throwback to the nineteenth century; in others, as with Dallapiccola and the rapidly growing list of atonalists, it is a modernized, nationalistically reoriented extension of Schönberg's twelve-tone theories, which are — both technically and spiritually — simply the next step beyond Strauss and Mahler in the development of central European Romanticism.

Stravinsky thus does not any longer exert a shaping influence upon new music or musical aesthetics in Europe (except upon Jean Françaix and some other French composers, most of whom belong in or near the orbit of Nadia Boulanger; and possibly upon Benjamin Britten and a few lesser figures in England). The United States has become more than his physical home; it is his artistic home as well. However controversial the merits of this piece or that may be, his significance in this country is inescapable. Here he continues to demonstrate to younger composers a model of craftsmanship and an unwavering sense of direction, and his own music finds a wider and more receptive following among musicians than that of the twelve-tone composers, of either the Schönberg and Alban Berg generation or that of Dallapiccola and Vogel.

Stravinsky's great contribution to the development of music in this country has been his clear exposition and demonstration of what musical classicism really is. One might suppose that we should have known all along what classicism is, but we have not. Nearly all our teaching in conservatory theory classes and college appreciation courses used to derive directly from the frozen formulations of late-nineteenth-century German pedagogues, given an even more glacial surface by such influential American adaptors as Percy Goetschius, in theory, and Walter Spalding or Daniel Gregory Mason, in appreciation.

Music, they taught us, consisted of two elements — form and content (or expression, or meaning). Form was man-made; content was God-given. To understand a Beethoven symphony you hunted for the first theme (which was masculine) and the second theme (which was feminine), along with whatever else there might be (heaven knew why) in the way of bridge passages, closing themes, codettas, and the like. You packaged all this neatly, calling it the Exposition, and then observed that these materials were "worked over" in a portion called the Development Section, and finally brought back, with the second theme in the tonic instead of the dominant key, in the part called the Recapitulation. This was called Analysis.

You then sat in rapt admiration of the wonderful beauties Beethoven, with the direct intervention of God, had festooned upon this loose-jointed skeleton, exclaiming that the climax of the development sounded as if the very heavens had opened, and likening the peaceful second theme to the quiet flow of the River Lethe. This was called Appreciation.

Stravinsky has been our strongest spokesman against this deeply imbedded notion that music is a dichotomy, with form and content two mutually exclusive elements that are somehow mystically wedded in great compositions. When he insisted, three decades ago, that the OCTUOR for wind instruments should be performed without attempts at expressive playing, he was endeavoring to make the point that form and content are not two things, but one. The expression, he maintains, resides in the form; the form of a piece of music is its meaning, and all the meaning it has (except, of course, when its scope is amplified by the use of words).

Musical form, consequently, cannot be achieved satisfactorily by following recipes given in textbooks. Every piece of music constitutes for its composer a fresh essay in the creation, not the mere filling out, of a form. The whole essence, the whole existence of a piece of music is found in the ordering of the notes (and rests) that constitute it. Every new piece is the product of a unique process that leads to a brand-new sequence of musical thoughts and a brand-new dynamism of musical events. Such a product, for Stravinsky, is a tangible object — devoid of supernatural hocus-pocus — designed to interest us entirely by the arrangement, relationship, and temporal movement of its materials. It is neither an exhortation toward a better life nor an emotional purgative. One should find pleasure in the character and operations of the music itself, not in its by-products and connotations.

To my taste, Stravinsky's aesthetic is set forth with unnecessary severity. It fails to take due cognizance of the highly affecting qualities his own music, along with all other successful examples of classically conceived "objective" music, cannot

212

help possessing. It is unnatural for any cultivated listener not to be moved by the orderly activity of musical tones, no matter how exclusively he devotes himself to the contemplation of the music and nothing else; and the emotional experiences rationally active tones produce are bound to relate themselves to other experiences, both musical and extra-musical, in our past and present lives, with a resultant excitation of our purely personal feelings.

But this objection — which I feel obliged to make in order merely to record it as a subject for tangential speculation — does not bear upon the present discussion. What matters to us here is Stravinsky's belief in the inseparable identity of structure and substance; for this belief is what makes him an upholder of the classic, as opposed to the Romantic tradition.

By a conscious intellectual process he has sought to recover, for himself and for contemporary music generally, the effortless unity of purpose that marked the works of Mozart and Haydn, and in large measure those of Beethoven and Schubert. When we think of Mozart's G Minor Symphony, we think of its musical materials, and of the continuity and proportion with which they are deployed. When we hear the symphony played, we want it to be played "straight"; no conductor can add anything to it by embellishing it with elaborate attempts at external expressiveness, for the music communicates its whole content without such devices. The good conductor of the G Minor Symphony is the one who can keep out of its way, enabling it to speak brightly, sweetly, and directly. When it is played in this fashion, it shows us how complete it is, how utterly felicitous in its solution of all its problems, how utterly unlike any other work by Mozart or by anyone else.

The only safe generalization about classical music is that it is not safe to generalize. When I was a young teacher, and a badly educated one, I used to mislead my students by telling them to hunt for the things they had told me at Harvard that I was expected to find. Privately, I was constantly worried because none of the symphonies or quartets or sonatas of Mozart or Haydn or Beethoven went through precisely the cut-and-dried processes I had been led to believe they all did (subject to the proviso, of course, that the great masters were privileged occasionally to break the rules). I wish Stravinsky had been my teacher, for he could have saved me the troubled years I spent discovering that the so-called rules were a mere card-index for pedants, and in no way corresponded to the volatility, initiative, and creative invention with which the classical composers accepted the challenge of making each work assume its shape in a new, something defiant, and usually wholly logical way.

"I cannot compose until I have determined what problem I must solve," Stravinsky has said. In this statement is implied his most valuable contribution to the American composer and the American listening audience. Music, he is insisting, is not rhetoric, not an attempt to elicit approbation or create excitement by fair means or foul. Music is logic; it presents its argument through the propriety with which its parts are related to a whole, living scheme. It will not wheedle us or overpower us, but will simply stand as an object for our enjoyment and gratification, if we have enough interest to identify ourselves with it.

Not every young and unproved composer, perhaps, can afford to emulate Stravinsky's calm aloofness and his disdain for the opinion of the mass audience. (Stravinsky himself does not maintain too Olympian a distance when there are attractive sums to be gotten from the circus or from Billy Rose — though such commercial commissions as these have not led him to relax his own standards of craftsmanship or to abandon his aesthetic convictions.) But no young American composer can afford to ignore Stravinsky's insistence that expression without cogent and congruent formal structure is not a proper musical aim. In the future battle between tonality and atonality, Stravinsky's principles will provide a desirable stabilizing force against too ready a capitulation to the new postwar Romanticism that is coming along, all decked out with twelve-tone rows. Stravinsky is able to distinguish what is essential to music from a great deal that is not essential, and perhaps not admissible. For this we owe him our attention and our respect.

16

D A V I D   H A L L

1949 Brief Note and Discography

In his *Chronicle of My Life* Igor Stravinsky takes an uncompromising position against "interpreters" of his music, contending, in effect, that the business of the players and of the conductor is to set forth the notes of his scores as written and without excrescences imposed upon them by a so-called "individual" approach. Given this point of view, it is not surprising that Stravinsky should have taken throughout his career an intense interest in the phonograph, not only as a means for wider dissemination of his creative work, but more particularly as a means of documenting accurately his own concepts of how his scores should sound. By the 1930's Igor Stravinsky's proficiency as a conductor had become truly expert, and at the same time technological progress in the art of recording was proceeding at a rapid pace. As a result, we have —beginning with the composer's initial recorded version of the SYMPHONY OF PSALMS (Columbia Album M-MM-162) — a series of superb musical and artistic documents in disc form, these being highlighted by the two versions of the SYMPHONY OF PSALMS, the augmented version of THE FIREBIRD, a great performance of THE RITE OF SPRING, the DUMBARTON OAKS CONCERTO and the SYMPHONY IN THREE MOVEMENTS. We can only voice regret that the composer has not yet (1949) given us his own complete performance of PETROUCHKA, and we hope that the time will come when the composer will conduct recorded performances of THE SOLDIER'S TALE complete with narrative, the SYMPHONIES OF WIND INSTRUMENTS, the wonderful OEDIPUS REX oratorio, PERSEPHONE and the SYMPHONY IN C. For the rest, Stravinsky's work is for the most part astoundingly well represented on discs, either under his own baton, or by other expert musicians. The stage pieces, REYNARD and MAVRA are the only other major omissions that come to our mind other than those already cited.

218

In the pages that follow, we have attempted to render a comprehensive discography of all the significant and extant recordings of Stravinsky's music. Where no other versions have been available, we have listed "cut-out" recordings. Likewise, when certain works have been available only in arrangements, we have listed them. Otherwise we have omitted both "deleted" discs and arrangements of works not done by the composer.

IGOR STRAVINSKY'S MUSIC ON RECORDS
(As of May 1, 1949; arranged in order of composition)

PASTORAL (wordless song for soprano and piano) (1907)
　　arr. Stravinsky for violin, oboe, English horn, clarinet
　　and bassoon
　Joseph Szigeti with Chamber Ensemble under
　Igor Stravinsky
　Columbia 72495-D, 12" Record
　Samuel Dushkin with Chamber Ensemble under
　Igor Stravinsky
　Columbia (England) LF129, 10" Record
　Philadelphia Orchestra under Leopold Stokowski
　Victor 1998, 10" Record
　　arr. Stravinsky for violin and piano
　Joseph Szigeti and Nikita de Magaloff
　Columbia 7304-M, 12" Record

FIREWORKS (fantasy for orchestra) (1908)
N. Y. Philharmonic-Symphony Orchestra under
Igor Stravinsky
Columbia 12459-D (in album M-MM-653), 12" Record
Chicago Symphony Orchestra under Desire Defauw
Victor 11-9447, 12" Record
EIAR Symphony Orchestra under Victor de Sabata
Cetra (Italy) PP60009, 12" Record
Berlin Philharmonic Orchestra under Erich Kleiber
Telefunken (Germany) SK1205; Ultraphon (Czecho-
slovakia) F14385, 12" Record

FOUR ETUDES (for piano) (1908)
Nos. 3 & 4 only
Soulima Stravinsky
Boite à Musique (France) 27, 12" Record
No. 4 only
Benno Moiseiwitsch
His Master's Voice (England) C2998, 12" Record

THE FIREBIRD (ballet in two tableaux) (1909-10)
Orchestral Suite (augmented 1946 version)
N. Y. Philharmonic-Symphony Orchestra under
Igor Stravinsky
Columbia ML4046, 12" Long Playing Record; Columbia
Album M-MM-653, Four 12" Records
Orchestral Suite (*Supplication of the Firebird* omitted)
London Philharmonic Orchestra under Ernest Ansermet
Decca (England) Album EDA-30, Three 12" Records
Orchestral Suite (*Supplication of the Firebird* and
Princesses' Game omitted)

220

Philharmonia Orchestra under Alceo Galliera
Columbia (England) DCX70/2, Three 12" Records
NBC Symphony Orchestra under Leopold Stokowski
(finale cut)
Victor Album M-DM-933, Three 12" Records
Philadelphia Orchestra under Leopold Stokowski
(finale cut)
Victor Album M-DM-291, Three 12" Records
All-American Orchestra under Leopold Stokowski
(finale cut)
Columbia Album M-MM-446, Three 12" Records
Berlin Philharmonic Orchestra under Oskar Fried
Polydor (France) 516650/1, Two 12" Records

PETROUCHKA (burlesque scenes in four tableaux) (1910-11)
London Philharmonic Orchestra under Ernest Ansermet
Decca (England) Album EDA-2, Five 12" Records
Philadelphia Orchestra under Leopold Stokowski
Victor Album M-DM-575, Four 12" Records
Symphony Orchestra under Igor Stravinsky
(*Dance of Ballerina and Moor* omitted)
Columbia (Italy) GQX10278/80, Three 12" Records
N. Y. Philharmonic-Symphony Orchestra under
Igor Stravinsky (includes only part of *Shrove-Tide Fair*,
plus *Russian Dance, In Petrouchka's Room* and concert
version of the *Grand Carnival*)
Columbia ML4047, 12" Long Playing Record; Columbia
Album X-MX-177, Two 12" Records

THE RITE OF SPRING (pictures of pagan Russia,
in two parts) (1911-13)
N. Y. Philharmonic-Symphony Orchestra under
Igor Stravinsky
Columbia ML4092, 12" Long Playing Record; Columbia
Album M-MM-417, Four 12" Records
San Francisco Symphony Orchestra under Pierre Monteux
Victor Album M-MM-1052, Four 12" Records
Amsterdam Concertgebouw Orchestra under
Eduard van Beinum
Decca (England) Album EDA-59, Four 12" Records
Philadelphia Orchestra under Leopold Stokowski
Victor Album M-DM-74, Four 12" Records

THE SONG OF THE NIGHTINGALE (symphonic poem)
(1909-17)
Cincinnati Symphony Orchestra under Eugene Goossens
Victor Album M-DM-1041, Four 12" Records

THREE PIECES FOR STRING QUARTET (1914)
Gordon String Quartet
Concert Hall Society Album B-6, Two 12" Records

THREE TALES FOR CHILDREN (for voice and piano)
(1915-17)
No. 1, only — Tilim-Bom
Alexander Kipnis (bass) with Celius Dougherty (piano)
Victor 15894, 12" Record

SONG OF THE VOLGA BOATMAN (arrangement) (1917)
Boston Symphony Orchestra under Serge Koussevitzky
Victor 15364 in Album M-DM-546, Two 12" Records

FIVE EASY PIECES FOR PIANO DUET (1917)
Arthur Gold and Robert Fizdale
Concert Hall Society Album A-6, Two 12″ Records

THE WEDDING (Russian choreographic scenes in four
tableaux) (1914-23)
Kate Winter (soprano), Linda Seymour (contralto),
Parry Jones (tenor), Roy Henderson (baritone) with
chorus, four pianos and percussion under Igor Stravinsky
Columbia Album M-MM-204, Three 12″ Records

THE SOLDIER'S TALE (to be read, played and
danced) (1918)
Concert Suite
Chamber Ensemble under Igor Stravinsky
Columbia Album M-MM-184, Three 12″ Records
Boston Symphony Chamber Ensemble under
Leonard Bernstein
In Victor Album M-DM-1197, Five 12″ Records

RAGTIME (for eleven instruments) (1918)
Chamber Ensemble under Igor Stravinsky
Columbia 68300-D, 12″ Record

PIANO RAG MUSIC (1919)
Igor Stravinsky
Columbia 68300-D, 12″ Record

THREE PIECES FOR CLARINET SOLO (1919)
Two pieces only
Ulysse Delécluse
Selmer SA 11, 12″ Record

PULCINELLA (ballet with songs in one tableaux after the
music of Pergolesi) (1919)
Suite for Small Orchestra
Symphony Orchestra under Igor Stravinsky
Columbia Album X-36, Two 12" Records
Suite Italienne (arr. 'cello and piano)
Raya Garbousova and Erich Itor-Kahn
Concert Hall Society Album C-5, Three 12" Records
Florence Hooton and Gerald Moore
Decca (England) X263/4, Two 12" Records
Serenade and Scherzino only (arr. violin and piano)
Samuel Dushkin and Igor Stravinsky
Columbia 68238-D (in Album M-199), 12" Record

CONCERTINO (in one movement, for string quartet) (1920)
Gordon String Quartet
Concert Hall Society Album B-6, Two 12" Records

SUITE NO. 2 (for small orchestra) (1915-21)
Danish State Radio Symphony Orchestra under
Nikolai Malko
His Master's Voice (England) Z297, 12" Record

MAVRA (1922)
Russian Maiden's Song (for violin and piano)
Joseph Szigeti and Igor Stravinsky
Columbia 72495-D, 12" Record

OCTET (for wind instruments) (1922-23)
    Chamber Ensemble under Igor Stravinsky
    Columbia Album X-MX-25, Two 12″ Records
    Boston Symphony Chamber Ensemble under
    Leonard Bernstein
    In Victor Album M-DM-1197, Five 12″ Records

CONCERTO (for piano and wind orchestra in three
    movements) (1923-24)
    Soulima Stravinsky with Paris Wind Instrument Society
    Orchestra under Fernand Oubradous
    His Master's Voice (France) DB11105/6, Two 12″ Records

SERENADE IN A (for piano in four movements) (1925)
    Igor Stravinsky
    Columbia (Italy) GQ7194/5, Two 10″ Records

APOLLO MUSAGETES (ballet in two tableaux for string
    orchestra) (1927-28)
    Boyd Neel String Orchestra under Boyd Neel
    Decca (England) X167/70, Three 12″ Records

THE FAIRY'S KISS (allegorical ballet in four tableaux inspired
    by the muse of Tchaikovsky) (1928)
        Divertimento (suite for orchestra)
    RCA Victor Symphony Orchestra under Igor Stravinsky
    Victor Album M-DM-1202, Three 12″ Records
        (arr. Samuel Dushkin) Ida Haendel (violin) and
        Ivor Newton (piano)
    Decca (England) Album EDA-109, Three 12″ Records

CAPRICCIO (for piano and orchestra in three
    movements) (1929)
    Jesus Maria Sanroma with the Boston Symphony Orchestra
    under Serge Koussevitzky
    Victor Album M-DM-685, Two 12″ Records
    Igor Stravinsky with the Straram Concerts Orchestra under
    Ernest Ansermet
    Columbia (Italy) GQX10519/20, 10556, Three 12″ Records

SYMPHONY OF PSALMS (for chorus of mixed voices and
    orchestra in three movements) (1930)
    Alexis Vlassof Choir and Straram Concerts Orchestra under
    Igor Stravinsky
    Columbia Album M-MM-162, Three 12″ Records
    CBS Symphony Orchestra and Chorus under Igor Stravinsky
    Columbia ML4129, 12″ Long Playing Record; Album
    M-MM-814, Three 12″ Records
    London Philharmonic Orchestra and Chorus under
    Ernest Ansermet
    Decca (England) Album EDA-52, Three 12″ Records

CONCERTO IN D (for violin and orchestra in four
    movements) (1931)
    Samuel Dushkin with the Lamoureux Orchestra under
    Igor Stravinsky
    Vox Album 173, Three 12″ Records

DUO CONCERTANT (for violin and piano in five
   movements) (1932)
   Samuel Dushkin and Igor Stravinsky
   Columbia Album M-199, Two 10, One 12" Records
   Joseph Szigeti and Igor Stravinsky
   Columbia Album (in preparation)

CONCERTO (for two solo pianos in four movements) (1935)
   Vera Appleton and Michael Field
   Vox Album 634, Three 12" Records

CARD PARTY (ballet in three deals) (1936)
   Berlin Philharmonic Orchestra under Igor Stravinsky
   Telefunken (Germany) SK2460/2; Ultraphon (Czecho-
   slovakia) G14244/6, Three 12" Records

CONCERTO IN E-FLAT "DUMBARTON OAKS"
   (for chamber orchestra) (1938)
   Dumbarton Oaks Festival Orchestra under Igor Stravinsky
   Mercury Album MDM-1; Keynote Album DM-1,
   Two 12" Records

   Hamburg State Philharmonic Chamber Orchestra under
   Hans Schmidt-Isserstedt
   Telefunken (Germany) E2994/5; Ultraphon (Czecho-
   slovakia) F18092/3, Two 12" Records

TANGO (for piano solo) (1940)
      arr. Victor Babin for two pianos
   Vitya Vronsky and Victor Babin
   Columbia 72084-D in Album M-MM-576, Three 12" Records

DANSES CONCERTANTES (for chamber orchestra of 24 instruments) (1941-42)
RCA Victor Symphony Orchestra under Igor Stravinsky
Victor Album M-DM-1234, Three 12" Records

CIRCUS POLKA (for the elephant ballet in the Barnum and Bailey Circus) (1942)
arr. Victor Babin for two pianos
Vitya Vronsky and Victor Babin
Columbia 72084-D in Album M-MM-576, Three 12" Records

FOUR NORWEGIAN MOODS (for orchestra) (1942)
N. Y. Philharmonic-Symphony Orchestra under
Igor Stravinsky
Columbia 12371-D, 12" Record

BABEL (cantata for reciter, male chorus and orchestra) (1944)
Edward Arnold with Chorus and Janssen Symphony
Orchestra of Los Angeles
In Artist Album JS-10, Five 12" Records

SCHERZO A LA RUSSE (1944)
RCA Victor Symphony Orchestra under Igor Stravinsky
In Victor Album M-DM-1234, Three 12" Records

BALLET SCENES (for orchestra) (1944)
N. Y. Philharmonic-Symphony Orchestra under
Igor Stravinsky
Columbia ML4047, 12" Long Playing Record; Album
X-MX-245, Two 12" Records

SONATA (for two pianos) (1943-4)
Arthur Gold and Robert Fizdale
Concert Hall Society Album A-6, Two 12" Records
Gino Gorini and Sergio Lorenzi
His Master's Voice (Italy) DB11308/9, Two 12" Records

SYMPHONY IN THREE MOVEMENTS (1945)
N. Y. Philharmonic-Symphony Orchestra under
Igor Stravinsky
Columbia ML4129, 12" Long Playing Record; Album
M-MM-680, Three 12" Records

EBONY CONCERTO (for Woody Herman's jazz
orchestra) (1945)
Woody Herman Band under Igor Stravinsky
Columbia 7479-M

CONCERTO IN D (for string orchestra) (1946)
Halle Orchestra under John Barbirolli
His Master's Voice (England) C3733/4, Two 12" Records

ORPHEUS (ballet) (1947)
RCA Victor Symphony Orchestra under Igor Stravinsky
Victor Album (in preparation)

MASS (for male choir and wind instruments) (1948)
RCA Victor Chorale and Orchestra under Igor Stravinsky
Victor Album (in preparation)

229

Fragment from "Orpheus"

17

Complete list of
the works of Stravinsky

(EXCLUSIVE OF THE VARIOUS ARRANGEMENTS FOR PIANO, VIOLIN, ETC.)

LITURGICAL:

1. Pater Noster (1926), Credo (1932), Ave Maria (1934)
   A Cappella mixed choruses in Russian for use in the
   Orthodox church.
   (a) Pater Noster and Ave Maria rearranged to Latin
   Text in March, 1949, for use in Roman Catholic church.

2. Mass (Kyrie, Gloria, Credo, Sanctus, Agnus Dei) for
   use in the Roman Catholic church — for 10 winds and
   mixed chorus (preferably male). Finished April 15, 1948.
   The Kyrie and Gloria were written in 1945. First performance under Ansermet, Milan, October 27, 1948.

WORKS WITH BIBLICAL TEXTS:

1. Symphonie of Psalms (1930) for large orchestra (sans
   violins, violas, clarinets) and mixed chorus (preferably
   male). First performance under Ansermet, Brussels,
   December 13, 1930.

2. Babel (1944) Cantata for orchestra male chorus and
   narrator. First performance under Werner Janssen, Los
   Angeles, 1945.

SONGS:

1. Le Faune et la Bergere — Suite of songs with
   orchestra   Pushkin
   (a) la Bergere; (b) Le Faune; (c) Le Torrent
   (mezzo soprano) First performance St. Petersburg,
   April 1906

2. Two Melodies for voice and piano (1907)   Gorodetsky
   (a) La Novice; (b) La Rosee Sainte

3. Pastorale for voice and piano (1908)

                                      Song Without Words

4. Two poems for Baritone and piano (1910)   Verlaine
   (a) Un Grand Sommeil Noir; (b) La Lune Blanche

5. Two Poesies for voice and piano (1911)   Balmont
   (a) Myosotis d'Amour Fleurette; (b) Le Pigeon

6. Three Japanese Lyrics (1913) for voice, piano, 2 flutes,
   2 clarinets, and string quartet.
   (a) Akahito; (b) Mazatsumi; (c) Tsaraiuki

7. Three Little Songs (souvenirs de mon enfance) for
   voice and piano (1913)
   (a) La Petite Pie; (b) Le Corbeau; (c) Tchitcher-Jatcher

8. Pribaoutki songs for voice, flute, oboe (Eng. Horn),
   clarinet, bassoon, violin, viola, cello, bass. (1914)
   (a) L'oncle Armand; (b) Le Four; (c) Le Colonel;
   (d) Le Vieux et le Lievre

9. Three Stories for Children (1915-17) for voice and piano
   (a) Tilimbom; (b) Le canard, les cygnes, les oies;
   (c) L'Ours

10. Berceuses du Chat (1915) songs for female voice and 3 clarinets
    (a) Sur le poele; (b) Interieure; (c) Dodo;
    (d) Ce qu'il a, le chat

11. Four Russian Songs (1918) for voice and piano
    (a) Canard; (b) Chanson pour Compter; (c) Le Moineau est Assis; (d) Chant Dissident

12. Four Russian Peasant Songs for female chorus (1914-17) (Saucers)
    (a) On Saints' Day in Chigisakh; (b) Ovsen; (c) The Pike; (d) Master Portly

    > *Note:* No. 9(a) was lengthened and orchestrated in 1923
    >
    > No. 3 was twice arranged by I.S. in 1923 for vl. and wind quartet

WORKS FOR TWO PIANOS:

1. Three Easy Pieces for piano duet (1915) March; Waltz; Polka
   Five Easy Pieces for piano duet (1917) Andante; Espanola; Balalaika; Napolitana; Galop

2. Concerto for Two Solo Pianos (1935)
   First performance by I.S. and Soulima Stravinsky Nov. 21, 1935, Paris

3. Sonata for Two Pianos (1943-4) First performance Nadia Boulanger and Richard Johnson at the Dominican Sisters, Madison, Wisconsin, July 1944

WORKS FOR POPULAR ORCHESTRA (with saxophones):

1. Tango (1940) for full orchestra plus 3 saxophones, guitar, piano.
   First performance under Benny Goodman, at Robin Hood Dell, July 1941

2. Scherzo a la Russe (1944) written for the Paul Whiteman Band
   Premier by Whiteman on broadcast

3. Praeludium (1945) unpublished

4. Ebony Concerto (1945) First performance by Walter Hendl and Woody Herman's Band at Carnegie Hall, March 25, 1946

WORKS FOR STRING QUARTET:

1. Three pieces for String Quartet (1914)

2. Concertino for String Quartet (1920)

WORKS FOR STRING ORCHESTRA:

1. Apollon Musagetes (1927-28) (Ballet)

2. Concerto in D (Basler) (1946)
   First performance in Basle. Paul Sacher conducted his orchestra

WORKS FOR WIND INSTRUMENTS:

1. Song of the Volga Boatmen (1917) orchestrated and arranged by Stravinsky

234

2. Symphonies of Wind Instruments (1920) First performance Koussevitsky, London, June 10, 1921. Revised version (1947) under Ansermet over NBC, 1948

3. Octuor (1923) First performance Oct. 18, 1923 in Paris, under Stravinsky

4. Three Pieces for Solo Clarinet. Played by Edmond Allegra, Lausanne, November 8, 1918

OPERAS: (3 acts)

1. Le Rossignol (1909-14) First performed in Paris, May 26, 1914. Emile Cooper, conductor.

2. Mavra (March, 1922) opera buffa in 1 act. First performed Paris, June 3, 1922, under Fitelberg.

3. The Rake's Progress (Act 1 finished Jan. 15, 1949)

BALLETS WITH VOICES:

1. Renard (1916) First performed June 3, 1922 in Paris under Ansermet.

2. Pulcinella (1920) First performed May 15, 1920 in Paris under Stravinsky.

3. Les Noces (1914-23) First performed June 13, 1923 in Paris under Ansermet.

BALLETS:

1. Firebird (1909-10) First performed June 25, 1910 in Paris under Pierne.

2. Petrouchka (1911) First performed June 13, 1911 under Monteux.

3. Le Sacre du Printemps (1912-13) First performed May 29, 1913 in Paris under Monteux.

4. Le Baiser de la Fee (1928) First performed Nov. 27, 1928 in Paris under Stravinsky.

5. Jeu de Cartes (1936) First performed New York, April 27, 1937 under Stravinsky.

6. Scenes de Ballet (1944) First performed 1944 in New York under Maurice Abravanel.

7. Ballet of Elephants (Circus Polka) (1942) Performed by Barnum & Bailey Circus, Spring 1942 in New York.

8. Orpheus (1947) First performed 1948 in New York by Stravinsky.

ORCHESTRAL WORKS AND SOLO PIECES WITH ORCHESTRA:

1. Symphony in Eb Opus 1. First performed St. Petersburg, Jan. 22, 1908

2. Scherzo Fantastic Opus 3. First performed St. Petersburg, Feb. 6, 1909, under Siloti.

3. Fireworks Opus 4. First performed St. Petersburg, June 17, 1908, under Siloti.

4. Funeral Dirge for the Death of Rimsky-Korsakoff (1908) Opus 5. Performed St. Petersburg in autumn of 1908. Unpublished.

5. Suites Nos. 1 & 2. Orchestrations of two piano works No. 1 (see above) Suite No. 1 performed Milan, June 17, 1926; suite No. 2 performed London, June 8, 1922 under Goossens.

6. Concerto for Piano and Wind Orchestra (1924) First performed May 22, 1924 under Koussevitsky. Pianist: Igor Stravinsky.

7. Capriccio for Piano and Orchestra (1929) First performed Dec. 6, 1929 under Ansermet. Pianist: Igor Stravinsky.

8. Violin Concerto (1931) First performed Oct. 23, 1931 in Berlin under Stravinsky. Soloist: Dushkin.

9. Symphony in C (1940) First performed Nov. 7, 1940, in Chicago under Stravinsky.

10. Four Norwegian Moods (1942) First performed January, 1944, in Boston under I.S.

11. Ode (1943) First performed Oct., 1943 in Boston under Koussevitsky.

12. Symphony in 3 Movements (1945) First performed Jan. 24, 1946 in New York under Stravinsky.

WORKS FOR FULL ORCHESTRA AND VOICES:

1. King of the Stars (1911) First performed 1938 in Brussels.

2. Oedipus Rex (1927) First performed May 30, 1927 in Paris under Stravinsky.

3. Persephone (1934) First performed April 30, 1934 in Paris under Stravinsky.

237

PIANO SOLOS, PIANO-VIOLIN AND VIOLA SOLO:

1. Piano Sonata (1904) unpublished.
2. Piano Sonata (1924)
3. Serenade en la (1925)
4. Four Etudes for Piano Opus 7 (1908)
5. Etude for Pianola (1917)
6. Piano Rag Music (1919)
7. Les Cinq Doigts — 8 Easy Pieces (1921)
8. Souvenir d'une Marche Boche (1915) Written at the suggestion of Henry James for Edith Wharton's *Livre de Sans Foyer*
9. Duo Concertante for Violin and Piano (1932)
10. Elegy (Prelude and Fugue for Unaccompanied Viola) First performed N. Y., 1946

CHAMBER MUSIC:

1. Rag Time for Eleven Instruments (1918) First performed 1925, in Paris under Stravinsky.
2. Concerto in Eb for Fifteen Instruments (Dumbarton Oaks) (1938) First performed in Washington, D. C. May 8, 1938, under Boulanger.
3. Danses Concertantes (1942) First performed Feb. 8, 1942 in Los Angeles under Stravinsky.
4. Histoire du Soldat (1918) for 7 instruments and narrator. First performed Sept. 28, 1918 in Lausanne under Ansermet.

   Note: Of the above works Stravinsky has made arrangements. The most important are:

1. Four Etudes for Orchestra, which are the 3 Pieces for String Quartet and the Pianola Etude now titled Madrid. First performed Nov. 7, 1930 under Ansermet.

2. Divertimento from Baiser de la Fee.

3. Symphony Orchestra arr. of Circus Polka, Scherzo a la Russe, Scenes de Ballet.

4. Firebird Suite — 1911, 1919, 1945 versions. Petrouchka revision 1947. Also 3 Movements for Piano Solo (1921). Sacre — last dance rewritten 1943.

5. About half of Pulcinella was made into a Suite, Rossignol, and a tone poem: Chant du Rossignol (1919). Violin, clarinet, piano version of Histoire du Soldat, also slightly shorter concert version.

ARRANGEMENTS BY STRAVINSKY:

The Kobold by Grieg for Nijinsky in Festin, 1909
Nocturne in Ab, Valse Brillante in Eb by Chopin, 1909
The Flea (1910) melodies by Beethoven and Moussorgsky
Various pieces and the Finale of Khovantschina (1913 — with Ravel)
Various numbers and an Entre-Acte for Sleeping Beauty (Tschaikovsky) 1921

In 1941 I.S. arranged the Pas de Deux (Bluebeard) from this original Sleeping Beauty arrangement for small orchestra.

Star Spangled Banner, 1941 — First performance by James Sample Oct. 14, 1941 in Los Angeles.

Acknowledgments to Original Edition

ARTICLES AND ESSAYS

ERIK SATIE. (From the first edition.) Reprinted from *Vanity Fair* by courtesy of the Conde Nast Publications, Inc.

JEAN COCTEAU. (From the first edition.) A portion of this article is reprinted from *Vanity Fair* by courtesy of the Conde Nast Publications, Inc.

HENRY BOYS. (From the first edition.) Reprinted by permission of the author and the *Monthly Musical Record*, London.

BORIS DE SCHLOEZER. (From the first edition.) Translated from the French by Ezra Pound. An abridgment selected from articles which appeared in the 1928-29 issues of *The Dial*.

EUGENE GOOSSENS. (From the first edition.) Written especially for the first edition of this book.

SIR OSBERT SITWELL. Paragraphs selected from *Great Morning*, Copyright 1947 by Sir Osbert Sitwell. Used by permission of the author, and Little, Brown & Co. *Atlantic Monthly Press.*

NICOLAS NABOKOFF. Article written for this book and the *Atlantic Monthly*. Used by courtesy of Edward Weeks and the *Atlantic Monthly*.

ARTHUR BERGER. Article used by courtesy of the author, and *Listen Magazine*.

AARON COPLAND
MERLE ARMITAGE
ROBERT CRAFT
SAMUEL DUSHKIN } written especially for this edition.
CECIL SMITH
LAWRENCE MORTON
DAVID HALL

PORTRAITS

Drawings by Marc Chagall, Russell Cowles and P. G. Napolitano were made especially for this edition. Early portrait by J. E. Blanche is from *The Russian Ballet in Western Europe*, courtesy The Bodley Head Ltd., London.

242

Photographic portraits by Edward Weston, Fred Plaut and Arnold Newman used by permission of the photographers. Photographs by John Vachon, courtesy *Look Magazine*. (Edward Weston photographs were used in the first edition of this book.)

REPRODUCTIONS

THREE MUSICIANS by Pablo Picasso. Private Collection. Courtesy of the Museum of Modern Art.

TAOS MOUNTAIN by Cady Wells. Used by courtesy of Cady Wells and the Durlacher Gallery, New York.

MUSIC by Paul Klee. From the Merle Armitage Collection.

FIRE BIRD by Antonio Frasconi. Used by permission of the Weyhe Gallery.

EXOTIC BIRD by Edward John Stevens, Jr. (End-sheet, rear.) Used by permission of the Weyhe Gallery.

FRAGMENT OF UNIVERSE by Carlus Dyer. (End-sheet, front.) Used by permission of the artist. Merle Armitage Collection.

CHAPTER HEAD DRAWINGS by Carlus Dyer. Fragments and themes taken from two drawings made for the first edition of this book. Ruth Maitland Collection.

DESIGNS

Title-page, colophon and other drawings were designed by Merle Armitage, and executed by Al Ewers.

Designed by Merle Armitage